Why Victorian Literature Still Matters

Blackwell Manifestos

In this new series major critics make timely interventions to address important concepts and subjects, including topics as diverse as, for example: Culture, Race, Religion, History, Society, Geography, Literature, Literary Theory, Shakespeare, Cinema, and Modernism. Written accessibly and with verve and spirit, these books follow no uniform prescription but set out to engage and challenge the broadest range of readers, from undergraduates to postgraduates, university teachers and general readers – all those, in short, interested in ongoing debates and controversies in the humanities and social sciences.

Already Published

Why Victorian Literature Still Matters

Philip Davis

WILEY-BLACKWELL

A John Wiley & Sons, Ltd., Publication

This edition first published 2008
© 2008 Philip Davis

Blackwell Publishing was acquired by John Wiley & Sons in February 2007. Blackwell's publishing program has been merged with Wiley's global Scientific, Technical, and Medical business to form Wiley-Blackwell.

Registered Office
John Wiley & Sons Ltd, The Atrium, Southern Gate, Chichester, West Sussex, PO19 8SQ, United Kingdom

Editorial Offices
350 Main Street, Malden, MA 02148-5020, USA
9600 Garsington Road, Oxford, OX4 2DQ, UK
The Atrium, Southern Gate, Chichester, West Sussex, PO19 8SQ, UK

For details of our global editorial offices, for customer services, and for information about how to apply for permission to reuse the copyright material in this book please see our website at www.wiley.com/wiley-blackwell.

The right of Philip Davis to be identified as the author of this work has been asserted in accordance with the Copyright, Designs and Patents Act 1988.

Library of Congress Cataloging-in-Publication Data

Davis, Philip (Philip Maurice)
    Why Victorian literature still matters / Philip Davis.
        p. cm.—(Blackwell manifestos)
    Includes bibliographical references and index.
    ISBN 978-1-4051-3578-8 (hardcover : alk. paper)—ISBN 978-1-4051-3579-5 (pbk. : alk. paper)
1. English fiction—19th century—History and criticism. 2. English literature—19th century—History and criticism. I. Title.

PR871.D35 2008
820.9′008—dc22
                                              2008009304

A catalogue record for this book is available from the British Library.

Set in 11.5/13.5pt Bembo by SPi Publisher Services, Pondicherry, India
Printed and bound in Singapore by Fabulous Printers Pte Ltd

1   2008

To all those associated with
The Reader and Get Into Reading

Contents

Introduction:
The Victorian Bump and
Where to Find It

Do not mention the "V" word. Don't talk about "the Victorians" en masse and their alleged views concerning Women or Society or the Lower Classes. Don't tell me what you are told they thought about Patriotism, The Family, Self-Help, Religion, or Morality – or, for that matter, anything else with a capital letter. Forget the ready-made categories that box-in experience. The great Victorians would point to areas, not names. "We lack, yet cannot fix upon the lack," wrote Christina Rossetti in "Later Life": "Not this, nor that; yet *somewhat*, certainly." "*The thing*" was palpably something there for Carlyle – the disturbance in the social world, whatever the name given it : "a matter in regard to which if something be not done, something will *do* itself one day."[1] These were felt realities, absent or present, without clear names.

Do not read as if what you read is merely past: it only distances you. Victoria's is the longest reign in English history, with accelerated change and burgeoning variety: 1830 is as different from 1880 as most so-called "ages" are from one another. So, do not even try to think historically as soon as you open a Victorian novel: it will become an all-too-knowing substitute for the experience of actual reading.

Don't speak of the Victorians' sentimentality – or of their emotional repression instead. Don't tell yourself that the book is merely pious or plain hypocritical.

Don't, don't, don't has the sound of hectoring prohibition, but really it is meant to be the language for a struggling freedom. These repetitions are a way only of saying what *not* to do, because people must not (and cannot really) be told, in advance, what they *should* do. You throw away the crutches offered by a semi-education – to find that you can walk after all. For all his own long-acquired learning, John Ruskin once planned to write an essay in defense of Ignorance.

With my friend and colleague Brian Nellist, I set up a part-time MA in Victorian literature long ago now in 1986 because we wanted a brave alternative community to that conventionally offered within a university institution. Over the years we attracted a large number of so-called mature students (meaning: enthusiastic and serious readers) from the ages of 22 to 72, of a variety of backgrounds, some of them without a first degree in English, a few without a first degree at all. They included secretaries, engineers, lawyers, social workers, teachers, librarians, midwives, retired booksellers, mothers at home with just enough time for themselves now that the children were at school. In those days it was the first part-time MA in arts and humanities in the North of England.

From the first, the "V" word was banned as a form of explanation. And that was because "Victorian" was not to be something to be anxiously learnt, a reassuring body of knowledge to be known, inertly, as context and background. Literature is not just a branch of social history; it is more (and more personal) than a receptacle of cultural and historical meaning. "Victorian" was rather something one *did*: it was a way of thinking and feeling. We could have denied, rightly of course, that "the Victorian" was simply one homogeneous thing: look at the variety of responses and points of view, consider the historical changes over 65 years. But what we were really interested in was that the individuals on the course should find their own instinctive and implicit sense of what Victorian literature meant for them. I have written a work that tries to give a balanced, relatively impersonal account of all that went on in literature between 1830 and 1880.[2] But this present little book is my version of what Victorian literature has meant for me not as an academic subject but as a form of being. My own equivalent to what I asked for from my students, it is the autobiography, if you like, of a neo-Victorian in which I break my own rule: I do use the V word and say, with partiality, what it means to me.

But I do stick to what was the only real rule on our MA: find what you positively *like* in a book. Tell me boldly what moves you, said Ruskin, and I will tell you who you are. Don't start people off, he said, telling them where to begin and what to begin with: find out, instead, where your people already start from.[3]

So we said to our students: think of something very specific, a little passage from a big book, that moves you – perhaps for a reason you cannot immediately give. Go for a walk without the book, as though it no longer existed in the world: what, after the initial blankness, are the fragments that come back to you? Those, involuntarily, are your chosen places, your good things, what Matthew Arnold called "touchstones."

Thinking of the book, without the book, in order then to return to it, is a wonderful thought-experiment, in order to find the real place of literature within a life. It is to do with losing the literal, and also with giving up on that equivocal privilege of simply taking the cultural for granted. In just that way, a teacher on a remote island gathers together the impoverished children after the soldiers have come from the mainland and cruelly burned their books. He announces a special rescue task – to retrieve *Great Expectations*. "Let's see if we can remember it," he said:

> We did not have to remember the story in any order or even as it really happened, but as it came to us. "You won't always remember at a convenient moment," he warned us. "It might come to you in the night. If so, you must hang onto that fragment until we meet in class. There, you can share it, and add it to the others. When we have gathered all the fragments we will put together the story. It will be as good as new."

What a responsibility we have, says that teacher, "to make sure that Dickens's great novel is not lost forever." One little girl in particular knows that responsibility as she struggles to hold onto her little recovered piece: "I was so terrified I would forget it. I didn't allow myself to be spoken to. I turned my head away from the other kids rather than risk my fragment make room for other thoughts and conversations." The teacher prefers it if the children can recall the exact words Dickens uses; otherwise he will settle for what he calls the "gist."

3

The little girl remembers Pip leaving his native village at dawn for his new life in the great city of London. He had been glad to go, moving onward and upward in the world. Then suddenly as he departed, he became tearful. No longer so sure about decisively going forward with his life, he almost turns around. But then he realizes he cannot go back. She remembers, simply and accurately: "It was now too late and too far to go back, so I went on."[4] Not quite choosing our own way, recalling too late what we have left behind, thus we go on toward adulthood. Later, this girl herself will leave this island.

But my MA people were not children on some remote South Pacific island. They were rather, for the most part, the ordinary adult inheritors of the great Victorian rise of the English middle class. However they had started out, they had arrived at some place of relative security, in the second stage of a life. This is perhaps *the* Victorian story, historically as well as personally, even as the turbulence of the 1830s and 1840s gave way to what has been called the age of equipoise in the third quarter of the century. In this story of establishment, you become middle-class, middle-aged, relatively comfortable and civilized: you become a sort of norm of the modernized world, with just sufficient freedom from immediately pressing necessities to make the questions of life askable if not answerable. "Normal" and "normality" are themselves Victorian words (though it is remarkable that Edgar Allan Poe, master of the uncanny, was one of the first deployers). In a normal world, the problems that concern you are not so much dramatic or romantic as continuous and probably unsolvable, because they are part of what is involved in accepting what Freud called the reality principle. "I loved my wife dearly, and I was happy," as one protagonist put it, entering life's second stage, "but the happiness I had vaguely anticipated, once, was not the happiness I enjoyed, and there was always something wanting." What is more, for him there had always been this lack – the old unhappy feeling "as undefined as ever." He cannot speak to his own wife about this, but writes his baffled honesty in secret, to himself:

> In fulfilment of the compact I have made with myself, to reflect my
> mind on this paper, I again examine it, closely, and bring its secrets to

the light. What I missed, I still regarded – I always regarded – as something that had been a dream of my youthful fancy; that was incapable of realization; that I was now discovering to be so, with some natural pain, as all men did. But that it would have been better for me if my wife could have helped me more, and shared the many thoughts in which I had no partner; and that this might have been; I knew.

Between these two irreconcilable conclusions: the one, that what I felt was general and unavoidable; the other, that it was particular to me, and might have been different: I balanced curiously, with no distinct sense of their opposition to each other. (Charles Dickens, *David Copperfield* (1850), ch. 48)

It is not an heroic black-and-white issue, it is a gray area that we are talking about here – not very bad, but not good enough either. And you live in that arena: that sad delayed verb "I knew" is what unavailingly you live with, even as you carry on with your lot. For it is a middle or middling life, at once defined from outside as that of the normal married man and yet still left unsatisfied, unsettled, and undefined within. It is a life uneasily placed in between the dreams of Romantic youth and the realities of Victorian adulthood; compromised between what all men must naturally relinquish and what nonetheless might have been different for me; and in the very midst of things, confused as to what is general and what particular in life, and baffled by how those two relate together. That is why the novel exists, when human beings are unsure of how life itself fits together. David Copperfield's is, he fears, the world of the sanely second best, still haunted by what seems both primary and yet impossible, and struggling as to how to take responsibility for itself. It is the world of realism inhabited by such as Tolstoy's Levin in *Anna Karenina*, living a sort of everyman's life distinguished only by the earnestness, honesty, and questioning bafflement with which he finds himself leading it. In the first days of his marriage (part 5, ch. 14), Levin feels like one who, after admiring safely from the shore the smooth, happy motion of a little boat upon the water, had now himself to get into the vessel. Whatever the ideas held beforehand, or the names given from outside, it is different inside – the golden rule of nineteenth-century experiential realism. Something strange is going on within something ostensibly familiar, something uncertain within something apparently safe, something personally big within something conventionally small.

That is how what is big keeps coming back again, within whatever forms it can find room for itself. There are powerful mythic stories of the time that seek to banish the great primary figures of instinct, tamed or sacrificed to the necessity of nineteenth-century civilization: Emily Brontë's *Wuthering Heights* (1847) is one, Thomas Hardy's *The Mayor of Casterbridge* (1886) another. The sensation novels of Wilkie Collins or Mary Elizabeth Braddon, with the murders and adulteries and disguises that appeal so much to postmodern critics in love with "the transgressive," are no less and no more than a thrilling, haunting sub-genre in reaction against that taming. But Heathcliff cries to the dying Catherine, "What *right* had you to leave me?" from a level of passional rights far deeper and earlier than that of altruistic considerateness (ch. 15). Whether it is Heathcliff with Linton or Henchard with Farfrae, the ancient figure could almost kill his smaller modern rival. But Henchard lets Farfrae go, finds he doesn't want to kill him only at the very moment when his hand is round the man's throat, when he suddenly remembers their past affection. A few hours later he goes after Farfrae again, not this time as murderer but as sudden make-shift messenger, to tell him that his wife (Henchard's former mistress) has unexpectedly become ill. But Farfrae, with his own view as to what is consistency, sees in Henchard only the would-be murderer again. "Henchard could almost feel this view of things in course of passage through Farfrae's mind." He asks himself: "Why had he not, before this, thought of what was only too obvious?" (ch. 40). These are figures who do not think "before this": they are from an earlier time, at once innocent and dangerous. Their fall is connected with the cutting down of the father-figure, the great patriarch, in so many Victorian stories from Dickens's Dombey and Father Dorrit to Samuel Butler's *The Way of All Flesh* (1903) and Arnold Bennett's *Clayhanger* (1910) in all the mixture of anger and pity that results. The nineteenth century, said John Henry Newman,[5] was heaven for small men but a purgatory for great ones. Why, for the sake of the social ordering, these primal disruptive beings must die — and with what mixture of loss and gain – is the story of Nietzsche's *Genealogy of Morals* (1887) and Freud's *Civilization and Its Discontents* (1930) – both of them, like Tolstoy's *Anna Karenina* (1877) or Kierkegaard's *The Sickness Unto Death* (1849), texts vital to the wider European context and meaning of the Victorian period.

But in such ways it is not merely a period; it stands for something deeper within the configuration of our psyches. "All public facts are to be individualized," said Emerson in his essay on "History," "all private facts are to be generalized": it works both ways, but always with the individual realization as crucial. The Victorians were interested in phrenology, the pseudo-science of studying bumps on the head, supposedly figuring certain localized areas and functions of the brain, such as a predominance to Benevolence or Destructiveness. Like ourselves, they wanted to map the brain, to try to see from outside what was happening within, and then use such external knowledge to modify the interrelations of the varying inner parts. I am saying here that there is, so to speak, a Victorian bump, a place in the mind that makes the experience of Victorian literature always matter.

And it is an in-between place: a place psychologically as well as historically in transition, moving back and forth ambivalently between the old and the new, the primal and the civilized, amidst a sense of gain and a fear of loss, and with the big questions constantly re-emerging and mutating within specific individual circumstances. In the last chapter of this book I will try to show the presence of "the Victorian bump" in works from or around the present. But if, before that, you want names, then the chapter that immediately follows from this introduction is about Morality and Toughness and the next, which goes with it, is about Religious Faith.[6] Yet really they are about the way Victorian literature *does* these things.

That "doing" is the subject of chapters 3, 4, and 5, on fictional prose, on poetry, and on non-fictional prose respectively and the presence of Victorian realism in all three. It is realism that is the great Victorian characteristic for me; realism that for so long in my life as a reluctantly so-called "academic" has been so unfashionable. Yet in the Victorian age there was a flowering of realism in literature as great as that in art in the late fifteenth and early sixteenth centuries, and itself crucial to a crisis in the Western conscience as to the very purposes of existence. There is much to be said about "realism," of course, and much that has been said often in complex theoretical writings – as to whether it is even possible or just another fictional illusion; as to how it relates to what is material and economic, and to what is physical and external; as to how it is involved in the implementation of ideals in practice. But I am interested above all in its relationship to ordinary life outside the world of writing; to problems of living life in a world of increasing secularization; and to questions about the existence of an external reality, or a higher truth, even if inside its structures I will never quite know or see it. Yet I simply start from just this, from within the period itself – George Henry Lewes in defense of realism in the *Fortnightly Review* (May–November 1865): "Fairies and demons, remote as they are from experience, are *not* created by a more vigorous effort of imagination than milkmaids and poachers." The imaginative power of a work, Lewes concluded, has been "too frequently estimated according to the extent of its *departure* from ordinary experience": realism meant high literature need not depart from ordinary experience but could find a base within it.

There are plenty of examples given in each chapter throughout this book for the reader to sample. Please don't read it just looking for the argument and skipping these examples, or thinking the consideration of them can be dismissed as academic "close reading." Everything important is lodged in the literary detail, the in-depth literary thinking, in tiny movements that are the necessary guise or disguise for big things passing too quickly under pressure of time and the limits of human realization. That is why this book is dedicated to the magazine and the outreach program that celebrate reading.[7]

1

Victorian Hard *Wiring*

Feeling for the Victorian "bump," we would often begin the part-time MA by reading early on, for example, Mrs Gaskell's *Ruth* (published in 1853). It is ostensibly the usual old Victorian story. Pretty young girl from the lower classes, seduced by young "gentleman," is left abandoned and pregnant. Just when she is on the point of drowning herself, however, a brother and sister take her in, and help her through the birth and the subsequent years of rearing her baby boy, passing her off as a young widow for the sake of social appearances. But of course, one day the so-called truth comes out, and suddenly Ruth finds that, before he hears it from the unkind lips of others, she has to tell her son Leonard, still no more than a boy, the one thing from which she had always shrunk as a parent – the true story of her sexual past. Here is the confession of mother to son that one person in the MA group, herself a single parent, naturally chose:

> Up they went into her own room. She drew him in, and bolted the door; and then, sitting down, she placed him (she had never let go of him) before her, holding him with her hands on each of his shoulders, and gazing into his face with a woeful look of the agony that could not find vent in words. At last she tried to speak; she tried with strong bodily effort, almost amounting to convulsion. But the words would not come; it was not till she saw the absolute terror depicted on his face that she found utterance; and then the sight of that terror changed the words from what she meant them to have been. She drew him to her, and laid her head upon his shoulder; hiding her face even there. (*Ruth*, ch. 27)

9

It is that rebounding sight of the boy's *absolute* terror that leaves her no room for her own fearful feelings. Collecting herself, she no longer hides her face but almost visibly takes on the responsibility – that forbidding Victorian word (responsibility!) suddenly made human:

> "Leonard!" said she at length, holding him away from her, and nerving herself up to tell him all by one spasmodic effort, "Listen to me."

Then she tells him that when she was very young she did very wrong. God, she believes, will judge her more tenderly than men. But still, she says, it was wrong in a way that Leonard will not understand yet. And even as she says it, "she saw the red flush come into his cheek, and it stung her as the first token of that shame which was to be his portion through life." People will call her the hardest names ever thrown at women:

> "and, my child, you must bear it patiently, because they will be partly right. Never get confused, by your love for me, into thinking that what I did was right ...
>
> "And Leonard," continued she, "this is not all. The punishment of punishments lies awaiting me still. It is to see you suffer for my wrongdoing. Yes, darling! they will speak shameful things of you, poor innocent child, as well as of me, who am guilty. They will throw it in your teeth through life, that your mother was never married – was not married when you were born –"

The punishment of punishments is for a parent to know that the mistakes of her youth – the very mistakes that made her a mother – have damaged the life of her child almost before it began, in a way that as a protective mother she herself would never have wanted or allowed. And that she has now to explain to the boy. It turns life back to front. You don't have to be a Victorian in that particular circumstance to have the imaginative emotion.

But think of "the Victorians" when you read this, and you may well think how characteristically unjust it is – in ways that the literature itself is only just beginning half to register – not only that Leonard should be stigmatized as illegitimate but also that Ruth should still blame herself for that. There is something indignantly important to be said about the way that social shame creates, unconsciously, a personal guilt and a misplaced sense of personal responsibility in an unhappily victimized woman, such as to redouble her injury. But the *reader* will also be noticing other things – for example, all the subtly implicit thought that is going on within the changing physical language of the sequence: Ruth never letting go of her boy, first holding him with her hands on his shoulders, while silently "*gazing into*" his face; then drawing him "*to*" her and "*hiding her face*" in his neck; then finally, holding him "*away*" from her as she begins to speak the all too adult, separating words.

It is by putting oneself into the tangle of these physical and emotional specifics that a great test comes upon a reader. In the modern world Ruth would have nothing for which to apologize, no terrible sense that her son could be labeled a bastard and herself a loose or fallen woman. Thankfully, the world of *Ruth* the novel has been left behind, made a painful historical document merely, in the subsequent march of social progress. For surely it would have been better here if Ruth could have carried out her task of explanation without the pain of thinking she had done wrong in her youth or that the people who now wrong her with cruel names "will be *partly* right"?

But in one sense it would *not* have been at all better: it would only have been easier. Undoubtedly that humane Unitarian Elizabeth Gaskell wanted more kindness in the world. But what moves Mrs Gaskell is not how her characters could imaginably get out of the temporary givenness of their situation but rather how they recommit themselves to staying within it and making something of it. It is not so much a feeling of guilt as a sense of primal responsibility that makes Ruth, regardless of extenuations, not seek finally to evade all the implications of her own story howsoever it has come upon her. Here this persistence depends upon Ruth having to believe that the position in which she finds herself is not wholly unjust, but a mixture of innocence in guilt. And though it is clearly wrong to her that her wrongdoing should have its effect upon Leonard's future life, still Leonard himself must not get confused, even by his love for her, into ever thinking that it was simply right. Seen from some humane political position far outside the novel, it may well be socio-historical pressure that makes her take that moral line against herself; but from within it, personally, and from within her, what motivates Ruth is love for Leonard, in the mother's care that the mother's own past example should not be his false moral standard. I love the way Ruth has to take that difficult double view of herself as both person and parent: in the personal feelings of her own private autobiography; in her overriding duty as a mother. That is what is so powerful about Victorian literature: the constant shift between vulnerable person and necessary function, in a world that must find its formal changes achieved even through informal and contingent means. In Dickens it is terrible when the great father-figure is revealed to his children as also a man in his own damaged right, embarrassing, vulnerable, or crudely culpable: it is a sudden and painful *rite de passage* that the age has to keep reliving.

The Victorian bump can feel hard. But what is hardest for the modern reader in this novel is that the imaginative situation would not be so deep here if Leonard *were* free of this unjust stigma. It is essential to the predicament. So: do we let children go on being called bastards and young girls slags because it produces better novels? Am I really saying that life is deeper when it was harder and we had what Mrs Thatcher used to call "Victorian values"?

Certainly it would be easier to be the man who saves Ruth from committing suicide, if he did not believe that she had committed a sin in becoming pregnant. But what is remarkable about Thurstan Benson is the way in which he finds himself rejoicing in the birth of Ruth's baby as a new life, even in the teeth of an argument with his own sister, Faith:

> "The sin appears to me to be quite distinct from its consequences."
> "Sophistry – and a temptation," said Miss Benson, decidedly.
> "No, it is not," said her brother, with equal decision. "In the eye of God, she is exactly the same as if the life she has led had left no trace behind. We knew her errors before, Faith."

"Yes, but not this disgrace – this badge of her shame!"

"Faith, Faith! Let me beg of you not to speak so of the little innocent babe, who may be God's messenger to lead her back to Him.
Think again of her first words – the burst of nature from her heart!
Did she not turn to God, and enter into a covenant with Him – 'I will
be so good'? Why, it draws her out of herself! If her life has hitherto
been self-seeking, and wickedly thoughtless, here is the very instrument to make her forget herself, and be thoughtful for another.
Teach her (and God will teach her, if man does not come between)
to reverence her child; and this reverence will shut out sin, – will be
purification."

He was very much excited; he was even surprised at his own excitement; but his thoughts and meditations through the long afternoon
had prepared his mind for this manner of viewing the subject.

"These are quite new ideas to me," said Miss Benson, coldly. "I think,
you, Thurstan, are the first person I ever heard rejoicing over the birth
of an illegitimate child. It appears to me, I must own, rather questionable
morality." (*Ruth*, ch. 11)

This is a "Victorian" religious language but not least because the situation is like a religious paradox: the disaster in Ruth's *first* life is also at
the self-same time the saving gift and triumph of her *second* – namely,
that she has become a mother. In George Eliot's *Silas Marner* (1861) a
child saves an adult's life, naturally, without intent or consciousness,
but there the bad father is split off from the good adoptive parent.
Here in *Ruth* what is good and what is bad are entangled. It would be
easier if there were no problem here; it would be easier if one had a
single, simple belief under which to categorize the situation. But
Benson, like Ruth herself later in confession to Leonard, has not one
but *two* powerful thoughts, at once inextricable and yet hardly compatible, the good-in-the-bad. These contrary pulls in the dense mix of
the Victorian realist novel are what produce between them something
humanly less definable and less predictable, making for the personal
individual achievement that is re-creative of a real morality. For this is
Benson acting more like Christ than like a Christian – the Christ
who surprised his over-literal disciples when he would not condemn
the woman taken in adultery or blame another who poured precious

ointment on his head instead of selling it to help the poor. Grace overcomes ethics narrowly conceived. It is in that very spirit that some of the greatest Victorians, such as Mrs Gaskell herself, are in a sense anti-Victorian, if Victorian only means such men as Mr Bradshaw in *Ruth*, the condemning Pharisee who likes to draw "a clear line of partition, which separated mankind into two great groups" – the saved and the damned (ch. 25). But Benson himself has no such clear lines, and it is telling that he was "very much excited; he was even surprised at his own excitement": that human response, transcending itself, is also what being a reader means, in going beyond any over-clear agenda.

This present book is thus for *the reader*, not "the critic" or "the student" or "the scholar" as such – though with the hope that the reader survives still within those other forms. For the Victorian is the first great age of nation-wide reading, Matthew Arnold insisting in his preface to *Culture and Anarchy* (1869) that it mattered not only *that* a person read every day but *what* the person read every day. Critics (even Arnold himself to a degree) are those who seek distance from the text, theoretical and historical, making it an object; but readers go to the book to internalize it, personally, emotionally, as if they might just find revealed there a version of the secrets of their lives.[1] That's why, to teach reading to an ordinary, serious community, the part-time MA that we first offered in Liverpool was in Victorian literature – because Victorian literature, and in particular the realist novel, is the most accessible of all, in terms of its commitment to a recognizably ordinary, mundane life. As such, it offers the portrait of such lives to real-life equivalents and identifiers as a form of emotional education.

Such reading is an immersed kind of thinking, different from other kinds of conceptualization, yet too often unrecognized as thinking. The reader first simply accepts the life-form in which the book exists, and then is absorbed in the people involved in it. The historical accidents of the predicament don't matter, save as clothing. For there are many ways in which a parent can harm a child's life without ever having wanted to do so; just as many as the ways in which children can be felt as a gift whatever the mess that engendered them. Good readers know that their deep, unsorted *memories* hold more of themselves than do their mere *ideas* of what they are. That is why they are glad to find a moment, a passage, in a literary work releasing feelings and triggering forgotten sympathies that surprise them with echoes that have lost, or never even held, a place in the limited frameworks of their conscious agendas. The emotion the reader feels *is* the immediate act of imagination here, the book's meaning existing simultaneously in front of the eyes and behind them. And thus with *Ruth* that affective sympathy, close to the novel's original intent and on the novel's own terms, is actually nearer to the past – precisely in so far as it is no longer felt as past, historically.

But the predicament is what matters, howsoever it arises, because what is moving is what human beings *do* with the given predicament, what the predicament as form brings out of those human beings as life's content. All the other, less individual ways of dealing with the predicament are history and are politics, but they are not literature.

That is no reason, of course, to let everything in the literal world outside books remain as it is, whatever the suffering or injustice. But equally, if you could imagine being able to remove all the predicaments in the world, it still might not be enough, and it might even be too much. And that last, famously, is the thought that precipitated the symbolic breakdown of the great program of nineteenth-century social reform in the person of its epitome, John Stuart Mill.

Almost from the cradle, Mill had been hot-house educated by his philosopher-father to become the great utilitarian social reformer. The son, as rational logician, was to make and to be that utopian future for which James Mill had worked in his own life-time. With that inherited master-scheme of increasing human happiness and abolishing human misery so firmly worked into his mind, the younger Mill recalls in his *Autobiography* how

> I was accustomed to felicitate myself on the certainty of a happy life which I enjoyed, through placing my happiness in something durable and distant, in which some progress might be always making, while it could never be exhausted by complete attainment.[2]

15

So the great Cause carried him along until he reached a prematurely tired adolescence. Then began the process that later left him asking in retrospect why, so unthinkingly, he had always needed the final goal of general human happiness to be ever distant, inexhaustible, and even unachievable. In the mental crisis of 1821, depression, with its questionings, came to Mill like a rite of passage between the movement away from the father and the emergence of an independent life:

> In this frame of mind it occurred to me to put the question directly to myself, "Suppose that all your objects in life were realized; that all the changes in institutions and opinions which you were looking forward to, could be completely effected at this very instant: would this be a great joy and happiness to you?" And an irrepressible self-consciousness distinctly answered, "No!" At this my heart sank within me: the whole foundation on which my life was constructed fell down. All my happiness was to have been found in the continual pursuit of this end. The end had ceased to charm, and how could there ever again be any interest in the means? I seemed to have nothing left to live for. (*Autobiography*, ch. 5)

He had relished the idea of the struggle for widespread reform, in the creation of a new and easier world, a new future with a new and happier form of human nature. But if ever, imaginably, that political struggle was completed – fulfilling itself in the utopian ending of *all* struggles for human beings – there would be for J. S. Mill nothing left in the dry resultant ease that was worth living for. The struggle, as means, was parasitic upon an end to which the reformer could look forward if indeed it never came. It was therefore sufficient as an "end" only in temporal terms, in the future-historical, not as an existential goal. The suddenly collapsed state in which Mill found his life cut short was, he said, like what he imagined it to be for converts to Methodism when smitten by their first conviction of sin. The great Victorians were unafraid of the great life-questions that in earlier ages had been put in religious terms – or rather, afraid, still put them, and often without help of religion. Yet in a secularized world Mill had no redemptive conversion available to him, equivalent to Methodism, not even in social politics. He had come to the verge of two radically

16

untenable realizations in terms of who he had been and what he had stood for – though later he shied away from them again. First: that a program of social and political reform was of itself, however useful and necessary, never sufficient in the fulfillment of human existence, and something else was also somehow needed. Second: that, illogically or paradoxically, the energy of human life always needed the very difficulties it sought to overcome, if it was not to decline into inertia. It was as though happiness or ease were not, perhaps, the goal or the purpose. Mill began to read poetry, in search of what was missing emotionally from his account of human existence.

★

In the background to reading the Victorians there is always something problematically tough, hard, and narrow, the demanding claims of which have either to be met or resisted. Its name was morality or conscience, insistent on the necessity of its place in the world because of the theology of the Fall. Laws, corrective rules, and guiding principles existed as a second nature, to compensate for the fallen ruin of our first nature. This is what in *Culture and Anarchy* (1869) Matthew Arnold was to identify as the stern Hebraic world-view, still strong in the first half of the nineteenth century, from the grim chains of which, in his view, a civilizing and cultured second half of the century had to free itself. It is what I am calling the hard wiring that underlines all subsequent mental modifications in the Victorian bump.

Here is an example of such stern demands taken from a minor and lesser-known novel, Elizabeth Sewell's *Journal of a Home Life* (1867). All you initially need to know about Miss Sewell is that the greatest influence in her life was her brother, and that William Sewell was a follower of Newman and Keble and Pusey in the Tractarian Movement, which sought to combat an age of increased secular liberalism through a strict high-church counter-reformation.

Miss Sewell's protagonist in *Home Life* is Mrs Anstruther, a widow by the time the book opens. She had not married the man she had first loved but instead at twenty-eight had given herself, in compassion, to someone old enough to be her father – a lonely, military man, whose first wife had died, leaving him with two little

17

girls called Ina and Cecil. When their father's career required him to return to his posting in South Africa, these girls were left in England to be raised by their maternal grandmother, Mrs Penrhyn, and sent to boarding school. In South Africa with a new wife, Colonel Anstruther raised a second family of four children. But on his death, after nearly 11 years away, Mary Anstruther returns to England not only with her own children but also with the added responsibility of the guardianship of the step-children who were left behind, now aged 15 and 13. This is a novel about being a parent and in particular a step-parent. It is like a novelist's recipe. Take some of what are to us the hardest, most unattractive of so-called "Victorian attitudes" in a parent (such as the need for discipline and morality). Only put them not into a forbidding patriarch such as Dombey but into a mother instead, a step-mother but not a wicked step-mother, a lonely woman who is absolutely devout in her sense of principles and responsibilities but also humanly affectionate, vulnerable, and herself in need of affection. Add in the crucial fact that the inherited children do need these uncomfortable disciplines, but also of course that they half-resist them. That is the mix.

"It seems," Mrs Anstruther writes to herself in her journal, "that the materials of life, like the constitution of the body, and the characteristics of the mind, are prepared for us, and we cannot alter them; but we may arrange them." If there ever was a primal world of absolute freedom and choice, for her it is now lost in the powerlessness of youthful fantasy and superseded by a second world of unchosen and circumscribed reality. From the large-scale freedom to plan and to change, there is a challenging shift to the restricted ability to arrange and manage:

> If there was one thing more than another which as a girl I resolved that I would never be, it was a step-mother. I had such a clear perception of the difficulties and awkwardnesses of the position; and, I remember, I used to argue about it furiously, and declare that it was unnatural — never intended; that it never could work for happiness; and a great deal more of the same kind; and the very first thing I did when I came to what are called years of discretion, was to marry a man with two children. (*Home Life*, ch. 29)

Life as thus depicted would be a grimly dutiful, ironically determined thing, were it not also so *unpredictably given* for acceptance. For the great challenging word here is "unnatural" – as if *that* was what the modern world increasingly felt like it was becoming. The social arrangements were moving beyond "nature," in being no longer governed or intended by the biology of a divinely created universe. Ina and Cecil were not Mrs Anstruther's natural children, and they were already more than half formed in their characters and habits by the time they were left in her charge. The children are not bad as such; it is nothing as dramatic as that. But they can't be left to carry on as they have been doing at boarding school – or rather they can so easily be – for they lie a little, they don't work very hard, they take their norms from their contemporaries. It is not long before Mrs Anstruther catches Ina casually making a social engagement without her guardian's consent, knowing it would not be given. It may not have been outright "deceit," Mrs Anstruther tells Ina, but in letting the thing happen it was an indirect version, a "shuffling" that characterizes her subsequent excuses:

> "I have never thought of that sort of thing being shuffling," said Ina; "we all did it at school. When we wanted to have our own way we managed to get it, that was all."
> "Precisely; that was all. Ina, dear, I want you to see how much there is contained in that expression 'that was all'. It means, to accustom ourselves to a low moral standard – to suppose that everything which is not absolutely wrong, is right." (*Home Life*, ch. 12)

For Mrs Anstruther a home should be a protection against these low social norms, a rectifying counter-tradition to "we all did it." But for Ina, morality is no more than a set of external rules, and of course the more strict the rules, the more she feels forced into shuffling. How to break that circle is Mrs Anstruther's problem. As a second mother she feels she is only, as it were, borrowing these children, while owing a responsibility for them not only to their recently lost father but to their long-dead mother, to both of whom they must be finally restored. But anything she can do in this charge can be done only by a mixture of sincerely willed duty and careful educative strategy – nothing can be simply loving, instinctual, easy, or unconscious in this second, artificial family. At her first reunion with Ina and Cecil, she speaks bravely and frankly of her own four children by their late father:

> I said laughingly, that they were little half brothers and sisters, who
> I hoped might some day become three-quarters, as they never could be
> whole ones; and just then I remarked that the two girls drew nearer to
> each other, as though tacitly consenting to the fact that no one could
> ever be to them what they were to each other. It goes against me to
> speak in this manner; I do so long to have my family all one; and these
> two elder children touch my heart in a way they can little imagine. But
> I will be patient, and lay the foundation of our mutual relations in the
> truth, and then the superstructure will be firm. (*Home Life,* ch. 3)

The sad truth that "goes against" the grain is that she never can be their natural mother and that with "these two elder children," the family is not naturally all one and whole.

It was that big old naming word "natural" that John Stuart Mill, as liberal progressivist and modernizer, had seized upon. Actually (he argued) "natural" was a word masquerading unconsciously in defense of what was often no more than socially ingrained "custom" and long-established "interests." Women, it was said, were "naturally" subordinate to men; the family was a "natural" institution – people felt it in their bones. And that is the difficulty that exists, said Mill in *The Subjection of Women* (1869), when the boldly rational reformer is contending against the irrationality of what has become through long association a deep, emotionally rooted prejudice; a prejudice claiming, moreover, to be natural feeling, instinctive belief, and traditional, plain common sense:

> So long as an opinion is strongly rooted in the feelings, it gains rather
> than loses in stability by having a preponderating weight of argument
> against it. For if it were accepted as a result of argument, the refutation
> of the argument might shake the solidity of the conviction; but when
> it rests solely on feeling, the worse it fares in argumentative contest, the
> more persuaded its adherents are that their feeling must have deeper
> ground, that the arguments do not reach; and while the feeling remains,

it is always throwing up fresh entrenchments of argument to repair any breach made in the old. (*Subjection of Women*, ch. 1)

Precisely because of our preconceptions, we do not know what human nature is, says Mill: we can only find out what it may *become* in experimenting toward a new future beyond traditional historical structures of society, gender, and family. In Hardy's *Jude the Obscure* (1895) there is even talk on Millite lines of raising children in some social commune instead. For Mill's is the challenge to the experiential authority of so-called natural feeling. And this too is the great value of the Victorian dilemma: namely, that there is no position in the period to which there is not an opposite offered in the ever-continuing conversations and shifting disputes of the age – in its melting-pot of the traditional and the modernizing held together at a crucial point in the formation of the Western conscience. (To Heathcliff – if we could imagine it across genres and categories – Mill would be like some super-intelligent version of Linton, a modern man in distorted denial of an incorrigibly demanding nature.) It is this that is the only important use of history for literature: that history should be made imaginably personal and present. *Doing* the Victorians, rather than merely knowing about them, involves imaginatively inhabiting in oneself as reader all that it means, personally, to exist in that often frightening transition between a world that seemed natural and one that had begun to go beyond such traditional bearings.

It also means struggling with the interrelation of the apparently large and the ostensibly small from the very inside of the process, at a point when the scale and place of almost everything in the mundane world seemed up for grabs. Poor Mrs Anstruther, for example, is embarrassed by her own excessive irritation when she hears some school-friends of Ina and Cecil whispering and giggling across the dinner table about their own concerns. It is rude of them but of course it is trivial. But however trivial in itself, it is a tendency and an example that Mrs Anstruther fears is ominous. And this is what parenthood can be like in the felt disproportions of practice – large, important principles trying to work themselves into small places without the clumsiness of undue anxiety.

21

So there is something large in the background to this anxious local commitment, when Mrs Anstruther takes on the final upbringing of her step-daughters. Indeed, that is the role of the largeness of morality or religion in such a world: that it should exist to emphasize the importance of its taking its place within the small. And the small here is the home life of a family-arrangement that represents, without great drama, what is awkwardly uncharted, relatively unprecedented, and almost anomalous. As a hybrid, this family in its mix of new and old would be for the reader of Mill the testing-ground for a genuine social, historical experiment. These two girls have not been brought up properly; they don't really understand morality or religion in an inward human sense, but only as abstractions. It is another part of the uncomfortable predicament that Mrs Anstruther comes to them at once late but not perhaps too late.

Ina in particular is not all that her step-mother would have her be. The problem in Mrs Anstruther's eyes is that Ina wants her own way and yet also wants to be liked and socially approved, to seem conventionally good and dutiful. This double need makes her duplicitous. "I do not, as yet, thoroughly understand Ina's character," the step-mother writes to herself in the journal that is her only counselor, "There is just something in it which gives me the idea of insincerity; but I am not a believer in insincerity as a motive, and I suspect that what appears to be so is rather a very determined self-will, which must carry its point, and when direct means fail, will choose those which are indirect" (*Home Life*, ch. 12). Direct untruth would be easier. The understanding of the psychologically *in*direct is what is so frightening. Mrs Anstruther can hardly bear to see how Ina will not be straight, in an attempted relation to truth, but too often is evasive and silent and passively secretive instead, in all the hidden willfulness of half-attempted freedom: "this easy glossing over what was wrong, twisting facts – not exactly dressing them up and exaggerating – but twisting, combining them, so as to form a pretty picture, the very antipode of reality" (ch. 9). To Mrs Anstruther there is a sort of cut-off unreality in Ina. Above all, what increasingly troubles the step-mother is self-deception, when *unknowingly* falsehood is taken as truth at a level that morality can hardly reach. "I have often felt certain she was deceiving herself," Mrs Anstruther writes of Ina, "and I am learning more and more to dread self-deception. I used to think that it was not compatible with truth in word or action, but I begin to believe that to a certain extent it is" (ch. 43). What makes Mrs Anstruther so disturbed is that the great Victorian threat to morality, here embodied in small anxieties, is not so much immorality any more but human psychology. If the nineteenth century is the great age of psychology, the significance of that fact is not decreased but enhanced by the recognition that for some Victorians, not entirely wrong-headedly, it was a deeply equivocal and unsettling achievement.

The increased awareness of psychology is part of that process of continuous adjustment and readjustment that is the inner drama of the Victorian story, in the effort to take nothing from either the importance of principle or the necessities of practice. In *Home Life*, there is a painful scene created when the obstinately interfering mother of the first Mrs Anstruther, Mrs Penrhyn, encourages impressionable young Ina to have to do with the charismatic Mrs Randolph. Mrs Randolph is not a bad woman, but she is living in a neurotic chaos of matrimonial disintegration. If the step-mother is struggling to create the right environment around Ina, then Mrs Randolph, whatever may be felt for her in her own situation, is potentially a damaging influence. These fears of laxness and bad example are easy of course to label "Victorian" and then dismiss as snobbish or priggish. But they remain in our background-memory of what being a guardian means, of what social influences can do, before we can dismiss the concerns as old-fashioned or over-protective. It is the same fear of moral miasma that Dickens's Little Dorrit feels when she sees her father, her brother, and her sister all succumbing to the prison mentality. At any rate, regardless of Mrs Anstruther's objections as to the undesirability of the association, Mrs Penrhyn slyly presumes to invite Mrs Randolph to stay in her house during the Christmas visit of Mrs Anstruther and the children, without prior warning. Mrs Randolph's visit being sprung upon Mrs Anstruther so unexpectedly, it is the indirectness that is so infuriating. As so often, Elizabeth Sewell is marvelous in registering her protagonist's anxious sense of bottled-up outrage forced to express itself as mere irritation. But she also reveals Mrs Anstruther's own concern as to how far that irritation is indeed petty – or is made so by the external disregard of the principles it struggles to stand for. Here is a long passage that I take to be just the sort of thing a merely casual modern reader – but not a real reader – would dismiss as old hat:

> Mrs. Penrhyn has treated me very badly. When I was talking to her the other day she ought to have told me that Mrs. Randolph was coming, even if she had not mentioned it before. And I have a suspicion – a very unpleasant one – that Ina has known of the invitation from the beginning, and has been told not to tell me. If it should be so – but I won't forestall worries – the question is, what am I to do – or rather, can I do any thing? If Mrs. Penrhyn does not choose to give me the ordinary confidence which I have a right to expect as the children's mother, and her guest, can I resent it? Am I bound to do so?
>
> I have a strong persuasion that if people don't keep their own place, and stand for what is their due, they bring themselves into difficulty; and I can plainly see the ill effect of this setting-me-aside process upon Ina's mind, how it tends to exalt her position in the family, and to make her look upon me as a person apart from it. And I might very fairly remonstrate with Mrs. Penrhyn – at least, show her that I was displeased. But I question much, whether I should do any good. If a neglect or rudeness – be it small or great – cannot be resented effectually, I suppose it is better to let it pass unnoticed. And, after all, the important point is, not how Mrs. Penrhyn acts or feels toward me, but what effect her conduct and Mrs. Randolph's coming will have upon Ina.
>
> With regard to this, I cannot say how powerless I feel. The little influence which I thought I had gained at home is entirely neutralized here. … It is in vain to fight against the inevitable. Mrs. Randolph shall come or go, without any remark from me. So also I will not inquire whether Ina knew of the visit and kept it from me. Ignorance is as often wisdom as it is bliss. I am not required to stand upon my right if I am not supposed to be aware that any right has been infringed; and if Ina were to tell me – as no doubt she would – that her grandmamma had forbidden her to mention that Mrs. Randolph was expected, I could say nothing – I could only look displeased, and so give the idea that I was jealous. (*Home Life*, ch. 26)

We would not normally have in this day the vocabulary or the syntax to make such a *fuss*, since that is what we would be tempted to think it. Yet its real name here is not fuss: that is to say, there is an imaginable world in which it stands for more than that. Only, it is as though what have been formal concerns, vital to human practice, are left without a language in a more informal society. What remains is only perhaps the muted background-feeling of vague, frustrated unease embarrassed by its own solicitude. Yet this is what novels can do long after the death of their authors and the lapsing of the times to which they refer: give, to what it would otherwise be so easy to dismiss in historical abstract as merely priggish or over-scrupulous, a sympathetic embodiment in a human situation and a human personality that makes the position emotionally imaginable. For Mrs Anstruther is here forced into the anomalous tension of private silence when the communal values she believes to be generally binding can find no particular space in her immediate world. That is what she means by trying to inhabit one's place and stand up for one's due, by a personal exemplification committed to make these beliefs still exist and physically count in the world. Yet what is intended as a humanely concerned defense of Ina's welfare is implicated in a power struggle: it makes for a context where the step-mother's attempt to salvage her own standing, for the sake of influence, is painfully vulnerable to being mistaken for egoistic jealousy — and indeed all too liable to become it. That is what happens when what is truly a *function*, embodied in a person, is treated by others in a less formal world as no more than merely personal. "I cannot say how powerless I feel." Her sheer embarrassment at the consciousness of how she is slighted and how she can be misinterpreted is given a place and a pained dignity in that alternative novel-world, between private and public, which is the realm of readers.

Almost always in Victorian literature there is still the presence of what I have called the hard thing – the Hebraic world, as Arnold called it, of harsh conditions and tough judgments, of struggle and of difficulty. "You have to stand up for yourself"; "Children must be brought up properly." To such as Arnold, literary man and educationalist, such maxims would be no more than crude and philistine talismans. And Dickens would know all too well what cruelty could be hidden within those slogans. But when a novel puts the (notionally) same thing into a different place, it is no longer the same thing at all, even though it may bear the same public name or is paraphrasable within the same general terms. We worry about "Victorian" parental attitudes, we want to let our children grow freely, we don't want to be untrusting of life or over-protective as to influences outside the home. But when I see the hard thing in Mrs Anstruther, tough and in difficulties in her effort to bring the children up properly, then I see something essential to parenthood in her predicament, howsoever it is particularly problematized. And I see another version of that struggling hard-core element, different again but related, in a greater novel, Anne Brontë's *The Tenant of Wildfell Hall* (1848). For there a wife who would just about manage to go along with the ways of her dissolute husband becomes a mother who cannot. At a deep primal level Helen Huntingdon fears the father's influence upon her boy – in both genetic and environmental terms, as we would call them – as she had not been able to fear the man's influence upon herself. But her absolute and transcendent need to counter the father's influence, and to provide what in abstract could be called a moral example, is compromised within the particular relative circumstances in which she finds herself:

> I am too grave to minister to his amusements and enter into his infantile sports as a nurse or a mother ought to do, and often his bursts of gleeful merriment trouble and alarm me; I see in them his father's spirit and temperament, and I tremble for the consequences; and, too often, damp the innocent mirth I ought to share. (*The Tenant of Wildfell Hall*, ch. 37)

The very syntax mimes the bitterly ironic configuration: that word "innocent" trapped in the very effort to protect it. But the father has no such weight of sad concern on his mind. He is light-hearted when he sees the boy, is good fun it seems, even offering sips of alcohol, while the mother looks on unattractively silent and worried:

> therefore, of course, the child dotes upon his seemingly joyous, amusing, ever indulgent papa, and will at any time gladly exchange my company

for his. This disturbs me greatly; not so much for the sake of my son's affection (though I do prize that highly, and though I feel it is my right, and know I have done much to earn it), as for that influence over him which, for his own advantage, I would strive to purchase and retain, and which for very spite his father delights to rob me of, and, from motives of mere idle egotism, is pleased to win to himself, making no use of it but to torment me, and ruin the child. (ch. 37)

You can feel through the syntax how the hard thing – the essential element, the necessary general principle – is battling to find a place for itself within this particular compound. That is always the task, as Iris Murdoch describes in her own tribute to the nineteenth-century novel: "How do the generalizations of philosophers connect with what I am doing in my day-to-day and moment-to-moment pilgrimage? ... My general being co-exists with my particular being. Fiction writers have, instinctively or reflectively, to solve the problems of this co-existence when they portray characters in books."[3] You could almost count how many different thoughts, coming from how many different levels or directions, there are in a single sentence that Helen Huntingdon writes in her lonely diary. "Not so much for the sake of my son's affection (though I do prize that highly, and though I feel it is my right, and know I have done much to earn it), as for that influence over him which, for his own advantage, I would strive to purchase and retain": three "though-type" clauses in a parenthesis, a "not so much" on one side matched by an "as for that" on the other, while the crucial "for his own advantage" seeks its rightful justificatory place within the overall sentence ... and so on.

Such relativism, especially in those who would be absolute in their principles, is what makes for an increasingly complicated syntax in the rich, dense life of the Victorian novel. It is a syntax that stands for the internal struggle toward an integrated, mapped-out orientation within the world – just as surely for George Eliot's Maggie Tulliver as for Helen Huntingdon or Mrs Anstruther. But Maggie is not an older woman struggling to apply single-minded, old principles in the face of an entangled new situation. She is a young girl baffled by the lack of emotionally meaningful connection in the painful raw materials of the world around her:

> She could make dream-worlds of her own – but no dream-world would satisfy her now. She wanted some explanation of this hard, real life: the unhappy-looking father, seated at the dull breakfast table; the childish, bewildered mother; the little sordid tasks that filled the hours, or the more oppressive emptiness of weary, joyless leisure; the need of some tender, demonstrative love; the cruel sense that Tom didn't mind what she thought or felt, and that they were no longer playfellows together; the privation of all pleasant things that had come to *her* more than to others: she wanted some key that would enable her to understand, and, in understanding, endure, the heavy weight that had fallen on her young heart. (*The Mill on the Floss* (1860), book 4, ch. 3)

This text is a list – father, mother, brother Tom, dull facts, hard tasks, painful gaps – in search of a syntax to make sense of this life, not in a dream-world but in this real one. Like a person, an initially simple sentence in the Victorian realist novel has to take in more and more. It tries to be receptive to the imagined world impinging upon it, to trace out the interrelations of clauses as of people, in the struggle for "some key" from within itself that would create connective understanding. But connective understanding does not mean that everything easily joins together. It has also to let in more difficult inclusions, syntactically close to contradiction or negation, such as David Copperfield's own pained admission "But that it would have been better for me if my wife could have helped me more … and that this might have been; I knew."[4]

"Oh, it is difficult, – life is very difficult!" cries Maggie toward the end of the novel, when she is torn in love between brother Tom and lover Stephen, between deep, past, familial ties and strong, sexually present ones:

> "It seems right to me sometimes that we should follow our strongest feeling; but then, such feelings continually come across the ties that all our former life has made for us, – the ties that have made others dependent on us, – and would cut them in two. If life were quite easy

and simple, as it might have been in Paradise, and we could always see
that one being first toward whom – I mean, if life did not make duties
for us before love comes, love would be a sign that two people ought
to belong to each other. But I see – I feel it is not so now." (*The Mill
on the Floss*, book 6, ch. 11)

In some primal paradisiacal world, thoughts would not "continually
come across" each other; the chronology of feelings would be in step
with their importance. But in this fallen Victorian second world, one
time, one thought, one person gets overlaid upon another, like threads
in a skein, like lenses through which we have to peer. One thought is
simple; two may be a contradiction or a conflict; but the generation
of three, four, five, and more are what creates the melting-pot, or the
holding-ground, or the deep reservoir of the realist novel, and demands
readers who do not seek merely a single theme, a simple idea. That is
why George Eliot's syntax has to be so complex, in its modeling of
the world, given how difficult it is even to make out an apparently
simple human creature such as pretty Hetty Sorel in her young
thoughtlessness: "Nature has her language ... but we don't know all
the intricacies of her syntax just yet, and in a hasty reading we may
happen to extract the very opposite of her real meaning" (*Adam Bede*
(1859), ch. 15) There can be no such hasty reading of George Eliot as,
in the ambition of Victorian high realism, she tries to lock into the
very syntax of the world's own complex composition. Intellectually,
George Eliot belonged with the liberal *Westminster Review* set of
rationalists such as Mill. But she knew how hard it was to deal with
complexity and as a novelist never did begin from a position of assured
intellectual achievement: her hard, single-minded figures such as
Maggie's brother Tom or Adam Bede himself can hardly bear the
uncertainties and anomalies. What always interests George Eliot is the
recurring moment of change, the renewed and renewing *rite de passage* of corrective realization, the difficulty of readjustment in that shift
of gear or focus that is never once and for all. As when (for example),
the ego of one human being rediscovers, as if for the first time, the real
presence of another person in the world – "the first stone against
which the pride of egoism stumbles is the *thou*, the *alter ego*"[5] – or

29

when a toughly tightened framework of understanding has to take in more than it can easily hold.

"No man is sufficient for the law which moral perfection sets before us," wrote Ludwig Feuerbach in the translation made by George Eliot, "but for that reason, neither is the law sufficient for man, for the heart."[6] The clash of rule and person, of criticism and affection, of judgment and grace, of morality and psychology: these are the mid-century struggles for balance that find supreme expression in George Eliot.

This is what happens when a greater writer takes up something of what Elizabeth Sewell represents. A young man goes to see his old mentor, the easy-going local vicar, in some desperation: Arthur wants to tell Mr Irwine that he has been tempted to do something wrong – to lead on and seduce an innocent young woman – so that in the act of telling the temptation will go away. It is like a memory of the ancient act of confession but now in a later, informal setting:

> there was this advantage in the old rigid forms, that they committed you to the fulfilment of a resolution by some outward deed: when you have put your mouth to one end of a hole in a stone wall, and are aware that there is an expectant ear at the other end, you are more likely to say what you came out with the intention of saying, than if you were seated with your legs in an easy attitude under the mahogany, with a companion who will have no reason to be surprised if you have nothing particular to say. (*Adam Bede*, ch. 16)

But the fact that the young man is in the presence of an old friend, who has no inkling of the serious internal struggle he has come to confide, shakes his own belief in the reality of its seriousness. Helping the evasion, there is a primitive feeling in Arthur that reality is only what is physical and external and present. "It was not, after all, a thing to make a fuss about": that "after all" is like Ina's "that was all," dismissing the reality of the moral dimension nagging away in his head. But when on the brink of confession Arthur pulls back from what previously he intended, George Eliot seizes upon the micro-moment, as if she were a super-version of that moral conscience that Arthur has at the last moment jettisoned from himself:

Was there a motive at work under this strange reluctance of Arthur's which had a sort of backstairs influence, not admitted to himself? Our mental business is carried on much in the same way as the business of the State: a great deal of hard work is done by agents who are not acknowledged. In a piece of machinery, too, I believe there is often a small unnoticeable wheel which has a great deal to do with the motion of the large obvious ones. Possibly, there was some such unrecognised agent secretly busy in Arthur's mind at this moment – possibly it was the fear lest he might hereafter find the fact of having made a confession to the Rector a serious annoyance, in case he should *not* be able quite to carry out his good resolutions. (*Adam Bede*, ch. 16)

The confessional has been taken away. There is no Mrs Anstruther, looking out for Ina. Instead, it is as with Jude in Hardy's *Jude the Obscure* when he most needs somebody advising him: "But nobody did come, because nobody does" (ch. 4). In place of confession, there is the novel with its discovery of what is now technically known as free indirect discourse: the inner mental language of the character released, without the character acknowledging it, into the language of the narrative. The realist novel does not put it "Arthur thought this or said that"; whatever he thinks, whatever he does not say, is simply exposed to sympathy, to judgment, to the world of readers.

But just because the presence of the moral teacher is taken away, it does not mean morality itself has gone with it. There is a famous letter from George Eliot to Frederic Harrison (August 15, 1866) on the role of moral didacticism in art:

That is a tremendously difficult problem which you have laid before me, and I think you see its difficulties, though they can hardly press upon you as they do on me, who have gone through again and again the severe effort of trying to make certain ideas thoroughly incarnate, as if they revealed themselves to me first in the flesh, and not in the spirit. I think aesthetic teaching is the highest of all teaching because it deals with life in its highest complexity. But if it ceases to be purely aesthetic – if it lapses anywhere from the picture to the diagram – it becomes the most offensive of all teaching. ... Consider the sort of

31

agonizing labour to an English-fed imagination to make art a sufficiently real back-ground, for the desired picture, to get breathing,
individual forms, and group them in the needful relations, so that the
presentation will lay hold on the emotions as human experience –
will, as you say, "flash" conviction on the world by means of aroused
sympathy.[7]

Take away the formal confessional and the physical confessor, and the
morality does not disappear but goes into psychology, as at some key
moment in the telling of the human story: in George Eliot's terms, the
idea and the spirit have to work within the individual flesh, and only
thus does the "diagram" become the "picture." With George Eliot,
wrote the Victorian man of letters John Morley, the reader with a conscience opens the book as though putting himself in the confessional.[8]
In adult life you can carry on going wrong: there may be no sign, no
person, to indicate even that it is wrong. That is how most of us manage
to get by, uneasily half let off the imperfections in an equivocal version
of freedom.

But still the novel in its own particular version of knowing silence
sits and watches characters such as Arthur evading confession "in case
he should *not* be able quite to carry out his good resolutions." Nobody
in real life ever wants to be exposed as Arthur is here by the novel
around him. But any reluctantly identifying reader with a memory
and a conscience is so exposed, silently, by proxy, as another of those
in-between characters who won't sacrifice the claims of their life to
the claims of morality and yet would not be immoral either. Through
silent immersion in the novel, in its silent inner replacement of the
ancient confessional, the reader finds in the human mind, here depicted
in Arthur, fear of the mind's own unacknowledged agents in the background – fear of the psychological small wheel that moves the more
cumbersomely obvious ones.

Arthur could have turned the threatened future into an articulated
thought that, made into an external marker, would have put an obsta-
cle in the way of that future's happening. Instead, precisely by not
anticipating the future in one way, he lets it happen in another, even
by pretending not to anticipate. In fact, he tacitly chooses not to let

this *present* become in the *future* a definite *past* whose promise he has broken. It is *that* complicated at the literary micro-level of the small internal wheels, however much at the cruder macro-level of ordinary human vocabulary we may call it simple "hypocrisy" or "evasion." In this George Eliot is like her researching doctor in *Middlemarch* who loves the imagination that "reveals subtle actions inaccessible by any sort of lens," tracking them by inward light through their long pathways in the dark:

> he wanted to pierce the obscurity of those minute processes which prepare human misery and joy, those invisible thoroughfares which are the first lurking-places of anguish, mania, and crime, that delicate poise and transition which determine the growth of happy or unhappy consciousness. (*Middlemarch*, ch. 16)

"Those minute processes," "those invisible thoroughfares," "that delicate poise and transition": this is the novel as analogous to research into the sub-structures of the brain. The realist imagination of the novel is not interested in fantasy but in finding deep within that ordinary named reality that we think we already know something stranger, more serious, and more complex than we ever thought it to be.

That is the picture, not the diagram. But in another sense a diagram does remain just visible behind the picture, as through X-ray vision. It is a diagram of hard wiring evolved out of hard times. For what the diagram here stands for, as part of our evolutionary template, is that underlying moral code of human purposiveness that the Victorians were, variously, losing, scared of losing, trying to retain, seeking to modify or to escape, wondering how to place. So many novels after 1850 re-create something of that old moral order in their first half, in order to see how to work through it in the second. Or a moralistic work such as Maria Edgeworth's *Helen* (1834) gets rewritten in a psychological form in Mrs Gaskell's *Wives and Daughters* (1866). In "Stanzas from the Grande Chartreuse", first published in 1855, Matthew Arnold famously spoke of living in a time "between two worlds," one well-nigh dead, the other still powerless to be born. The Victorian bump exists equivalently between old and new, between tough and tolerant, between absolute and relative, between belief and unbelief. Held in such tense transition between the two worlds, it is for us, I am saying, no longer history as such but the site of a dilemma that will not ease itself by simply letting go of one out of any two important alternatives. It won't let go of either, and we should not let go of it. "I have often thought it is part of the inner system of this earth," says the protagonist of J. A. Froude's *The Nemesis of Faith* (1849), "that each one of us should repeat over again in his own experience the spiritual condition of its antecedent eras."

2

Isaiah and Ezekiel – But What About Charley?

Here is a vision – entitled "Dining with the Prophets" – that could only be Romantic in its sheer personal nerve:

> The Prophets Isaiah and Ezekiel dined with me, and I asked them how they dared so roundly to assert that God spake to them; and whether they did not think at the time, that they would be misunderstood, & so be the cause of imposition.
>
> Isaiah answered: I saw no God, nor heard any, in a finite organical perception; but my senses discovered the infinite in every thing, and as I was then persuaded & remain confirmed that the voice of honest indignation is the voice of God, I cared not for consequences but wrote.
>
> Then I asked: does a firm persuasion that a thing is so, make it so?
>
> He replied: All poets believe that it does, & in ages of imagination this firm persuasion removed mountains; but many are not capable of a firm persuasion of any thing.[1]

It is of course William Blake, from *The Marriage of Heaven and Hell* (1790), speaking in what the poet wills to be his own Age of Imagination – that is to say: an age in which you could naturally *believe* in what you imagined, and not merely think that you *only imagined* it. But there is also another side of Blake in the satiric voice of the teasing, rational skeptic who asks with apparent naivety: "Does a firm persuasion that a thing *is* so, *make* it so?"

In post-Romantic times, most people might agree that the truth of a thought is not to be measured by the innocent subjective intensity

35

with which it is held or asserted. The poet in Blake can find a liberated place in his *own* created world where, as he again puts it in *The Marriage of Heaven and Hell*, "every thing possible to be believed is an image of truth" – where subjective belief can have its own objective power; where everything possible to be believed holds some truth somewhere and in some way. But to a post-Romantic, even to think that a belief holds good in it is not the same as being able to have that belief. As John Stuart Mill put it, in the midst of his nervous break-down: "To know that a feeling would make me happy if I had it, did not give me the feeling."[2] This acknowledgement is not just to do with helplessness: scrupulousness too may mean the necessity of suspecting the good that may come from a belief that is really a comforting illusion.

You are told that "firm persuasion" can move mountains. But the prophets add that many are not capable of that firm persuasion. What do you do if you are not Isaiah or Ezekiel, but one of those many? Take the case where it is not simply that you disbelieve: on the con-trary, you believe in belief, its power, its confidence, but you don't seem to *have* any. How do you go about *getting* belief? Belief in *what* exactly? And is it a belief at all, if you have to try to get it?

I am going to call such reluctant non-believers *Charley* – for reasons that will become clear later. When it comes to the all too well-known Victorian debate between faith and doubt, the Charleys occupy the uncomfortable territory in between straightforward belief and out-right disbelief, as if they had no choice but to make it habitable. They are sincere and vulnerable agnostics – the word "agnosticism" itself strategically coined by the aggressive Darwinist T. H. Huxley in 1869 to avoid the imputation of atheism.

If we trace his history, Charley does not belong in Blake's 1790s but dates from George Eliot's 1850s. Imagine Charley having to hear this, from Feuerbach's *Essence of Christianity*, which George Eliot translated when she was Marian Evans:

> That which the unreligious man holds in his head merely, the religious man places out of and above himself as an object, and hence recognises in himself the relation of a formal subordination. The religious man

has an aim. Only activity with a purpose, which is the union of theo-retic and practical activity, gives man a moral basis and support, *i.e.,* character. Every man, therefore, must place before himself a God, *i.e.,* an aim, a purpose. He who has an aim has a law over him; he does not merely guide himself; he is guided. He who has no aim, has no home, no sanctuary; aimlessness is the greatest unhappiness. An aim sets limits; but limits are the mentors of virtue. He who has an aim has a religion.[3]

This must seem a well-nigh secular version of what is a religion, of what is a God. It tries to rescue the phenomenon of belief (which is humanly valuable, like confidence) from belief in God (who is man-made and otherwise non-existent). With Feuerbach anything, poten-tially, can be the object of belief: in place of the one transcendent God, there is now the necessary risk of true or false human gods such as politics, money, love, kindness, private life. To Feuerbach you could choose – and consciously or unconsciously you always do have to choose – your own ground of being, in need of some justification for a life. But even so, the pressure on Charley is severe. For if belief can be in anything, with all that worrying arbitrariness, still it must not be in nothing. Feuerbach's demanding challenge is that if you do not believe in anything, then you are not a real person, of founded char-acter. And if your life has no real purpose, then deep down you will be unhappy. So, Charley, what do *you* believe in and what is *your* ulti-mate aim?

No wonder our Charley, with his religious hangover, believes in the importance of belief and feels weakened by not being able to give witness. Under such social and historical pressure, what is remarkable is not so much that Charley does not *know* if he has anything match-ing up to that belief; what is impressive is rather that he dare admit that he may have none. These Charleys, wondering what they will do without God, may be denigrated by untroubled believers as indeci-sive, overly cerebral, lacking in strength of feeling or resolve. But the Charleys are intelligent and scrupulous people, not least because their intelligence has the integrity to stand relatively free of any allegiance. They see that what *unreligious* people know they have made up inside their heads, *religious* people unconsciously place outside themselves, as though to make those meanings somehow more real. Human beings often do not want to guide themselves; traditionally they have wanted to feel guided. That is why, to Charley, all our religions, all our beliefs may really be subjective and fictional projections, which, of course, we do not want to discover to be so. Others may fend it off, but the great underlying fear of the age that surfaces in such as Charley is that conviction may be no more than an unconscious psychological defense against uncertainty, freedom, and loneliness.

There is an easy way out beckoning here. We could say: this is the trouble with the Victorian age, this is its historical dilemma in the transition toward a more full-blown, adult secularization – namely, that by a vicious circle, the more the conditions for belief became unpropitious, the more the pressure to retain some version of such belief symptomatically increased. The greater the fear of no-belief, the greater the pressure to produce that fiction of belief. And the greater that pressure to believe, the less chance of believing – at least amongst those, like Charley, who wanted sincerely to do so *without* succumbing to fictional make-believe. They conscientiously wanted their faith to come from within, when the pressure to believe was simultaneously coming from without. Thus they had to fight against what outside forces were demanding, even as inside themselves they wanted the self-same thing but in a genuinely achieved form. Charleys wanted their beliefs to be neither an unconscious form of coerced and dutiful social conformity nor a fiction projected out of their own individual psychological neediness. In the same way, in the alternations of *In Memoriam* (1850) Tennyson feared his desire to believe but, for all that, did still want to believe, and yet do so not merely as a psychological refuge from despair.

Was not all this to set the bar of faith too high? As Henry Scott Holland puts it, in *Lux Mundi*, looking back at his century from 1889:

Now faith, under rapid and stormy challenges, is apt to fall into panic. For this, surely, is the very meaning of panic – a fear that feeds upon itself. Men in a panic are frightened at finding themselves afraid. So now with faith: it is terrified at its own alarm. ... If our faith were real faith (we say), would it ever lose its confidence? To be frightened is to confess itself false: for faith is confidence in God, Who can never fail. How can faith allow of doubt or hesitation?[4]

And so, says Scott Holland, a whole generation talked itself into distrusting and then abandoning their faith in God not just because of a crisis of confidence, but more because they thought they shouldn't be having such a crisis at all, if they were true believers. They should have been to cope with Biblical criticism, with the rise of Darwinism, with increased materialism: these were formidable challenges but not fatal ones. But under the pressure of over-high demands, these Charleys believed that the very fact of *having* a crisis of doubt was incompatible with belief, was already a sign of the inner failure of not believing.

Yet however overbearing or even counter-productive the anxious pressures to believe, perhaps they had an urgent rightness in them in one respect at least: that not to believe in any sustaining ground for existence was indeed a human disaster. It is no use simply blaming external Victorian pressures. The pressures were there anyway, and should be, inside any life that seeks and questions direction, purpose, and meaning. The American psychologist William James, brother of the novelist Henry James, came to Edinburgh to give the Gifford lectures on religion between 1899 and 1901. There in the first lecture of what became *The Varieties of Religious Experience* he sought to retell those stories that gave "a true record of great-souled persons wrestling with the crises of their fate." *That* – the wrestling and the need – was the first religious impulse, and deserving of the name religious howsoever it was subsequently resolved. The religious impulse seemed to James central to the human psyche, whatever the form of the personal experience of it.

I am saying that, in the same spirit, we need to take seriously the phenomenon of "wanting to believe" – the position characteristic of some Victorian struggles in being caught between believing and not believing. It seems undoubtedly less impressive than the crises that William James describes in Bunyan or Tolstoy. It suffers from being a secondary or second-order condition – wanting to believe seems weak, hankering, left over. And, equally, it seems to belong not to an age of faith or an age of imagination but to an age of self-consciousness (and the Victorians were themselves often somewhat comforted by these descriptions of their historical position). So Carlyle writes in his great essay "Characteristics" (1831) that "the healthy know not of their health"; it is only the sick who are conscious of the desirability of healthiness.[5] For indeed, ironically enough for the sick, the sign of health is *un*consciousness, a certain primary spontaneity of being and of doing. Ages of action and of heroism and of belief are not ages of moral philosophy, says Carlyle. As soon as something has ceased to be an involuntary part of a whole way of being, and has had instead to become separately aware of itself, and argued over, then, says Carlyle, it is already in decline. Self-consciousness is what comes afterward, comes second because it is secondary, and is itself the symptom of disease, even while seeking its own cure. Thus, in a vicious circle, wanting-to-believe is an ironic and fallen condition because there would not be this want-as-desire if there were not, lurking behind it, the want-as-lack.

It is this second-order condition that is occupied above all in the mid-Victorian period by Arthur Hugh Clough, the basis for Claude in his poem "Amours de Voyage" (1858). In one of the poem's drafts his sensible friend Eustace writes to Claude, saying that Claude's intellectual doubt is all too much the product of inaction, of living always in the scrupulous beforehand: "Action involves belief," writes Eustace, "Act and all will be clear."[6] But in the final version of the poem Claude himself writes:

> *Action will furnish belief,* – but will that belief be the true one?
> That is the point, you know. However, it doesn't much matter.
> What one wants, I suppose, is to predetermine the action,
> So as to make it entail, not a chance-belief, but the true one.
> (*Amours de Voyage*, 5.2)

It is the same here as it is in Clough's "Dipsychus" (1865) – both warn that the mid-Victorian stress on the priority of action, on the cold shower of practical duty, may have degenerated into a version of an anti-intellectual PE master at Rugby School. For what Dipsychus, like Claude, insists upon is that the rush to practical action might be a form of giving up and selling out; that action might itself be a fear of hesitation and a flight from waiting; and thus, above all, that action ironically might be a form not of belief but of despair, sacrificing a larger hope you cannot seem to realize to a smaller practical gain you immediately can, instead. Get over it, get on with it, throw yourself into it. But all too automatically, action *will* furnish belief, think Clough's men, and then you become what you have done, not out of first principles or true belief but through chance belief and knock-on effects – the thought automatically following the action rather than truly producing it. The sheer autonomous rational intelligence of Clough is characterized by its no longer being, as it were, in time with time. For intelligence is what steps out of the temporal sequence, and by the sheer force of extraordinary intellect turns the sequence round in one's head to get at what lies behind it:

Action will furnish belief, – but will that belief be the true one?

In a notebook of 1849, written partly in Rome and partly in Liverpool, Clough commented upon what he called the wrong doctrine of habits: – such that by doing acts *like* those of love, we shall indeed come to love. To Clough this was mechanical habituation – getting soldiers into the way of marching by means of music, schoolboys into the way of thinking by learning off by heart, husbands into the way of loving by giving their wives flowers.[7] The establishment of a virtuous "hexis" or disposition, by acts of repetitive habit, was the way classically prescribed by Aristotle. It was a way of working from outside in. The religious would adopt set habits of devotion, rather than wait till the rare occasions when the spirit spontaneously moved them, in order to make themselves into what in a fallen condition they all too rarely were of their own accord. But to Clough this was increasingly degenerating into a form of what he called Victorian virtue-manufacture. In search of truth rather than relief, Claude does not want to be the slave of action or conditioning. Desperate for sincerity, fearful of factiously creating in himself what might not be there

41

of its own accord, Claude is a would-be idealist, a disappointed Platonist who seeks within this realm of the secondary the lost world of truth's primacy, and is obliged to try out complicated strategies in order to turn it all round:

> What one wants, I suppose, is to predetermine the action
> So as to make it entail, not a chance-belief, but the true one.

Yet there may be no true belief, and the idea of a pristine world of truth may only be created by what is felt as missing in this fallen one.

"He does not even love God second-hand," complains a young woman in *Wilfrid Cumbermede*, a novel of 1872 written by that great, uneven, and still neglected genius George MacDonald. To which another character replies, "Perhaps because he is very anxious to love him first-hand."[8]

The person they are talking about is called Charley, Charley Osborne — the name I chose for the type instead of Claude. Charley is the son of a stern, remorseless evangelical. The pressure for him does not come from "Victorian Society" but in the more intimately confusing form of the parent–child relationship. As Wilfrid Cumbermede, Charley's friend, says of the hard father:

> A good man I do not doubt he was; but he did the hard parts of his duty to the neglect of his genial parts, and therefore was not a man to help others to be good. His own son revived the moment he took his leave of us — began to open up as the little red flower called the Shepherd's Hour-Glass opens when the cloud withdraws. It is a terrible thing when the father is the cloud, and not the sun, of his child's life. (ch. 16)

That is why there is no first base or ground for such children, even as they grow. The demanding father that remains inside Charley himself *wants* to believe, in that wistfully fallen derivative of faith. But the damaged filial part of Charley cannot simply believe, and in the beginnings of its autonomy cannot even trust the wanting to, in all its mere secondariness. It is easier of course if Charley simply dishes the religion with the father; but what if the father is only a confusingly wrong version, the twisted personal form, of what may still be somewhere right? "From his father," says Cumbermede, Charley like some impotent modern hybrid "had inherited a conscience of abnormal sensibility; but he could not inherit the religious dogmas by means of which his father had partly deadened, had partly distorted his" (ch. 16).

You don't get on with your father. You don't believe in anything. The Victorian challenge insists that those two things go together, and together they mean you may be a lost person. It is out of something like those hard pre-Freudian thoughts that George Eliot writes *Daniel Deronda* (1876).

At one crisis point the spiritually disinherited Charley cries out to his friend, desperately, "If there *were* a God – that is, if I were sure there was a God, Wilfrid!" Wilfrid has to try to find a reply to this almost unfinished sentence:

> I could not answer. How could I? *I* had never seen God, as the old story says Moses did on the clouded mountain. All I could return was,
> "I suppose there should be a God, Charley! – Mightn't there be a God!"
> "I don't know," he returned. "How should *I* know whether there *might* be a God?"
> "But *may* there not be a *might be*?" I rejoined ...
> I do not mean this was exactly what he or I said. Unable to recall the words themselves, I put the sense of the thing in as clear a shape as I can. (ch. 21)

That is what George MacDonald most wanted – not to give the reality a reduced, second-order name, but to find it a place or a shape that the imagination could inhabit. The "may be a might be" offers within a tight spot a linguistically hard-won chink of possibility, doubling the conditionals in creative defiance of the accusation of lame, yearning weakness. Are such formulations as "But *may* there not be a *might be*?" *always* an easy indulgence – or are they not, on the contrary, sometimes as here a great risk, a wonderful verbal effort at holding on as by the fingertips of writing? In their very different ways Søren Kierkegaard and John Henry Newman staked their existence in the nineteenth

43

century on the predication that we were naturally *doing* creatures, not *doubting* creatures, and that what we always did was risk our feelings and beliefs and actions without absolute surety. "If we are intended for great ends," says Newman, "we are called to great hazards; and, whereas we are given absolute certainty in nothing, we must in all things choose between doubt and inactivity."[9] What is more, for all the strenuous efforts of skeptical intellect, it was vanity to suppose it was somehow harder *not* to believe. The tougher risk – the work of what Kierkegaard called "a humble courage to dare" – was to believe that the individual was indeed called to a relation to God.[10]

Yet Charley still says to Wilfrid that the worst of all possible miseries would be to believe in a lovely thing and then find that, after all, it was not true.

> "You might never find it out, though," I said. "You might be able to comfort yourself with it all your life."
> "I was wrong," he cried fiercely, "Never to find it out would be the hell of all hells." (ch. 35)

The delusion was the hell of hells, even while you thought it was heaven. This is Charley's impossible thought – refusing a delusion that you would not know if you had it. It is the other side of the position Clough himself for once achieved by the end of his "Hymnos Ahymnos," saying to God:

> Be thou but there, in soul and heart,
> I will not ask to feel thou art.

Here indeed are the two great impossible thoughts of religious dilemma: I don't feel God is there but he is; I think God is there but he is not. And both of them are beyond the limits of thought, are double thoughts we cannot really think or wholly avoid either, and need literature even to imagine.

In his respect for a God he cannot believe in but will not falsify, how can it be that this Charley, potentially the most religious of persons, could not be religious at all? Is there something wrong with him, or is there something wrong with what religion is taken to be? What

44

do you call Charley's refusal of a comforting fiction that he might never find out to be a fiction? All this is like a preparation for something that after all may never happen – as if *that* might be what life itself extendedly is for such people, left by their own scrupulous intelligence hanging in the realm of unresolvable possibility, without decision or action.

Almost every academic or intellectual I know likes to talk of Keats's "negative capability," from his famous letter of December 21, 1817, to George and Thomas Keats: "that is when man is capable of being in uncertainties, Mysteries, doubts without any irritable reaching after fact & reason." But I am not sure that we can or should long hold positions of sustained neutrality. There is a cruelty or a desperation involved in forcing the premature taking of sides. But, equally, there is an abuse of intellectual freedom when all that negative capability serves is a refusal of what its freedom is *for*. Everything is a decision at some point. If we are, biologically, feeling and believing and doing creatures, as Newman argues, with all the attendant risks, then unharnessed intelligence is in danger of being notional, of putting us above ourselves. It is William James who takes on the Victorian heritage in these matters, when in 1895 in a talk at Harvard on W. H. Mallock's fine book *Is Life Worth Living?* he speaks of intelligence's neutrality as finally *unsustainable*:

> This is because, as the psychologists tell us, belief and doubt are living attitudes, and involve conduct on our part. Our only way, for example, of doubting, or refusing to believe, that a certain thing *is*, is continuing to act as if it were *not*. ... If I doubt that you are worthy of my confidence, I keep you uninformed of all my secrets just as if you were *un*worthy of the same. If I doubt the need of insuring my house, I leave it uninsured as much as if I believed there were no need. And so if I must not believe that the world is divine, I can only express that refusal by declining ever to act distinctively as if it were so, which can only mean acting on certain critical occasions as if it were *not* so, or in an irreligious way. There are, you see, inevitable occasions in life when inaction is a kind of action, and not to be for is to be practically against; and in all such cases strict and consistent neutrality is an unattainable thing.[11]

What William James offers instead of a self-damaging scrupulosity held safe in a world of literary ambiguity is the venturing position of "as if." In lecture 3 of *The Varieties of Religious Experience* (1902) he writes of how "we can act *as if* there were a God; feel *as if* we were free; consider Nature *as if* she were full of special designs; lay plans *as if* we were to be immortal; and we find then that these words do make a genuine difference in our mortal life."[12] I call this position a venture because it involves what James calls "going with ideas upon which we can ride" – ideas that seem to create a vitality in us and make for greater possible movement into a future. They are called thoughts or ideas, because their "as if" dynamically frees them from the pressure of their having to be called beliefs in static certainty. For let us be clear about the pragmatism of these *as ifs*: like George MacDonald's "may be a might be," they are instrumental and provisional, essays in the very process of our making ourselves do more and be more and go further than we might dare in advance. "I am well aware," says James in "What Pragmatism Means," "how odd it must seem to some of you to hear me say that an idea is 'true' so long as it is profitable to our lives … Ought we ever not to believe what it is better for us to believe?"[13]

That is James's bold proposition: if a thought energizes, somehow making life work better, there must be something in it. Is not this, however, precisely what Clough would dismiss as "truth" turned merely into comfortable convenience – the sustaining illusion of fiction, the self-deception of fantasy? But I do not think it is: James does not simply choose a belief because it is comfortable. His point is rather that if it works, there must be something literally vital in it because "belief and doubt are living attitudes." And living attitudes are such by lighting up the brain, by changing its very temperature and configuration:

> We have a thought, or we perform an act, repeatedly, but on a certain day the real meaning of the thought peals through us for the first time, or the act has suddenly turned into a moral impossibility. All we know is that there are dead feelings, dead ideas, and cold beliefs, and there are hot and live ones; and when one grows hot and alive within us, everything has to re-crystallize about it. (*The Varieties of Religious Experience*, lecture 9).

46

That change suggests the opening of a pathway not only within the brain but outside it, a way forward suddenly intuited. And this is why pragmatism is a venture, a narrative that replaces "thinking before" with "following through," a testing out of a living future for an idea, because pragmatism is not only to do with results but with a radical change in orientation. That is to say: pragmatism is "the attitude of looking away from first things, principles, 'categories', supposed necessities; and of looking towards last things, fruits, consequences, facts" (*Selected Writings*, p. 8). There is no going back to check where the thought has come from, but rather a going on with where it may be leading to. It is a route therefore in which one trusts important first principles to come into play eventually, as part of biological or organic development, rather than in anterior abstract planning. It offers – "in its abandonment of the claim to see the world from the stars, its embrace of the awkward situation of the human agent, struggling against institutional and conceptual structures that shackle him, its offer to help him loosen and reinvent these structures so that he may become greater and more vital as well as less deluded" – the chance to make a real-life story, feeling one's way forward in intuitive development of an opening ahead.[14]

In William James's life what pragmatism was about was a son's fight against youthful depression. As a young man, on the verge of a breakdown, he had looked at the world and wondered whether he could believe in the life it seemed to offer. The world could look like a mere machine of which its inhabitants were no more than determined parts. Nonetheless, whether this was true or not, James did recognize that he himself was already an additional subjective element in the equation he was trying to make out in advance. That is to say: his depression at the very least contributed to his sense of determinism as well as arising out of it. If this was plausible, then conversely the first act of freedom might be to risk believing in freedom itself. He is writing to his past, young self when he later says in "Is Life Worth Living?": "Your mistrust of life has removed whatever worth your own enduring existence might have given it" (*The Will to Believe and Other Essays*, p. 60). Think of a train robbery, he writes: a whole train of passengers may be robbed by a few highwaymen simply because the highwaymen can count on one another, while each passenger separately fears that if he makes a movement of resistance he will be shot before anyone backs him up. That fear and doubt and want of collective confidence are what give the robbers their power. "There are, then, cases where a fact cannot come at all unless a preliminary faith exists in its coming ... *where faith in a fact can create the fact*" (*Selected Writings*, p. 265). That is what is wrong with taking oneself out of the account in apparent neutrality. The subject – what you are and what you make of yourself – has also its part to play in the summing of the objective whole. This is for James the great moment, the great transformation from mere defeated sadness, when suddenly you realize that paradoxical gift of responsibility and shift into that second gear that you can find in yourself. The difference you feel you need, for life to be worthwhile, is already *there* as a nascent element of dissatisfaction that exists in *you*. Define life, but remember that our own reactions upon the world, small as they are in bulk, are *themselves* "integral parts of the whole thing, and necessarily help to determine the definition." "Believe that life *is* worth living, and your belief will help create the fact" (*The Will to Believe and Other Essays*, p. 62). Above all then, this makes wanting-to-believe not merely secondary, wistful, or untrustworthy: it makes wanting-to-believe itself a form of personally risked belief – through the route created by "as if." It expresses belief in human "need" – need registered not as defeat but as aspiration.

Indeed, James goes so far as to say that this personal sense of want may be how what we call "God" works, with God coming into being in the world through our flawed personal need for him. Charley thinks he needs an external or higher validation for a sense of belief to be certain and true. But it may be we only need the imagination of such a sanction in order to change the world a little. If that is so, we couldn't at once exercise that imagination *and* be conscious that that *was* what we were doing, without returning to Charley's fear that our faith was a fiction. It may be that it doesn't matter. What we can do for ourselves, even if we have to call that God – even if it *is* God – we must do in whatever ways we find we have to. But I say again, as though to Charley: these aren't thoughts that, in our limitation, we can really think.

It is at that point of limit that theology is powerful – in particular, for the nineteenth century, two theological works that are written precisely on that boundary of human understanding. They are H. L. Mansel's *The Limits of Religious Thought*, the Bampton lectures for 1858, and the book that Mansel acknowledges as lying behind it, Bishop Joseph Butler's *Analogy* (1736). Both these works, for all their ostensibly austere rationality, are secret books, works consisting in two parts – of which only the first part is written. In each, the first part, written on *this* side of our limits, concerns both the attempt to think and the inability to accomplish that attempt. In each the act of reason is undertaken precisely to show reason's own limitations. These books speak to the sense that our whole consciousness is compassed about with restrictions that we are ever striving to pass, and ever failing in the effort. Both Butler and Mansel insist that the very experience of this limitation implies something on the *other* side of it, the very inadequacy of reason pointing to some higher truth, of which the inadequacy indicates the existence but does not make known the substance.

And the second part? The second part if written would be mystical, but is not there. The second part is left secret, implied, and unwritten on the other side of the first, with everything left in place there by remaining silent about it. That secret book might say, with James, that God himself allows us to create him in our own way. It might argue that whatever we as creatures can creatively believe in is, as for Blake, an image of truth however distorted or mishandled. To Feuerbach of course, it was always we who did it, we who made the difference, even though we have had to think it was God who was responsible. We *are* God, says Feuerbach; unconsciously we made him; and the divine attributes are really the best of human ones, projected upon a fictive Other. Feuerbach says to Charley or to Claude: why can't we now go onward, pointing the creativity of our previously religiously ordered gifts and values no longer out toward God but back to our own purely secular, human ends?

But I am saying instead, with William James, that we should not be too sure of what is human and what is religious, or where our best things come from. I started with that deep sentence of

49

Feuerbach's: "That which the unreligious man holds in his head merely, the religious man places out of and above himself as an object." To this, William James adds one crucial consideration with which I must end. And it is this: that, after all, the religious person may be right about our essential experience of thinking – that it does not just exist in our heads. Of course, thinking exists in our own heads if it is no more than the putting of thoughts into ready-made names and categories. But James hates *that* kind of thinking, which still, I fear, dominates even the study of literature: neat, tamed, uncreative, and pigeon-holingly thematic or contextual. He loves instead what he calls "the unclassified residuum," a literary sort of thinking that in him goes on outside literature itself. To George MacDonald, for example, in his own struggles against Charley, when a new thought arises in the mind, a person is rather *being thought* than thinking. And the best thing that Nature did for Wordsworth, says MacDonald, and that Wordsworth does for us, is to put a human being into that mood or condition or space or shape in which thoughts come of themselves. Thoughts are not ours.[15] To James, likewise, in our real thinking we do not make thoughts, but thoughts in some sense come to us, not felt as originating in ourselves but experienced *as if* constituting a demand or a gift or a necessity from somewhere else. And such thoughts exist in us precisely to refer us toward what they stand for outside ourselves, blurring just that boundary between the person who has them and the things they themselves point to. It is as though we are the bar of iron James describes as follows:

> It is as if a bar of iron, without touch or sight, with no representative faculty whatever, might nevertheless be strongly endowed with an inner capacity for magnetic feeling; and as if, through the various arousals of its magnetism by magnets coming and going in its neighbourhood, it might be consciously determined to different attitudes and tendencies. Such a bar of iron could never give you an outward description of the agencies that had the power of stirring it so strongly; yet of their presence, and of their significance for its life, it would be intensely aware through every fibre of its being. (*The Varieties of Religious Experience*, lecture 3)

There we are, like blind and dumb things, sensing a field of forces and energies around us in which we are involved. The brain is suddenly magnetized by a thought. Without yet understanding the thought, the brain nonetheless *recognizes* it, like a neurological sensor registering a deep passional excitement prior to conceptualization and unexhausted by it. When the thoughts that come light up the brain as if they were beliefs, then we are in the process of seeing how important they are, by seeing how far forward they can take us, how far they can work for the making of life, what they do for us in mind and affect.

Yet when Thomas Hardy read William James's vitalist dictum, "Truth is what works," he wrote in his notebook that a worse abuse of language had never been perpetrated: truth to Hardy was all that did *not* work.[16] For such as Hardy, a belief might be precisely what does not make for life, might be reluctantly negative, in the name of a tough truth that goes against the grain of all our warmest human feelings and ignores them. Human life might not be supported by anything in the universe save chance; life itself might be intrinsically disappointing. That Hardyesque possibility was part of James's struggle against depression, to work within and struggle against such considerations, to see what if anything was still resiliently left in us when we tried to accept them. That is the inescapable challenge that Thomas Hardy reluctantly stands for in the century. But at some level, James himself implicitly believed that belief itself had always, finally, to be a faith in an ultimate *good* in the universe, which the very belief helps exist. Reading James really does give you just that feeling he describes – the feeling of thoughts generating live excitement, energy, heat, change – whatever the pain or difficulty of their specific content. It is "as if" those thoughts were a response to something that Doris Lessing in her "Canopus in Argos" series of space fictions calls Need – Need, which includes a sense not only of neediness but also of necessity. These vitalizing thoughts feel called for: that's the wager.

It is above all the act of writing that is the most genuine form of thinking in terms of trying out what works. And by that I mean writing, like James's own, which does not know in advance where it is quite going, where it is taking us. James's "as if" and MacDonald's "may be a might be" are syntactical instruments that create space for

51

a dynamic form of writing, not knowing in advance the way or shape it is trying out. As one of James's own disciples, John Dewey, put it:

> Different ideas have their different "feels," their immediate qualitative aspect, just as much as anything else. One who is thinking his way through a complicated problem finds direction in his way by means of this property of ideas. Their qualities stop him when he enters the wrong path and send him ahead when he hits the right one. They are signs of an intellectual "Stop and go." If a thinker had to work out the meaning of such ideas discursively, he would be lost in a labyrinth that had no end and no centre.[17]

That is what creative writing should mean. And it is what creative thinking does mean, finally, in George MacDonald, transcending Charley.

For in his great, strange, final work *Lilith* (1895), perhaps the greatest of the nearly lost, unjustly neglected texts of Victorian Britain, MacDonald makes faith and doubt alike creative. There toward the end, MacDonald's protagonist finds himself waking alone in the house of the dead where he has fallen asleep, and walks out into a suddenly lovely landscape. There he meets Adam, father of mankind, who tells him that he is dreaming this, that he is still asleep in the chamber of the dead, with the dead all around him, awaiting resurrection. "I am trying hard to believe you, father," says MacDonald's hero, but here *in* the dream is someone saying that it *is* a dream. Is that someone real, a counter to the dream, or just another part of it? "I am trying hard to believe." To which Adam replies, "You are not to blame that you cannot ... Thou doubtest because thou lovest the truth," adding in appreciation of the struggling effort: "Because even in a dream you believe me, I will help you" (ch. 43).

MacDonald's man does not know whether he is awake or dreaming. "To myself I seemed wide awake, but I believed I was in a dream because he told me so." But he says: "Even in a dream the dreamer must do something! He cannot sit down and refuse to stir until the dream grow weary of him and depart: I took up my wandering" (ch. 43). Whatever it is in which he finds himself, it has to be lived through as a reality. You think you are alive, but someone tells you are really lying in the house of the dead. You feel awake but someone tells you that you are dreaming. Back and forth it goes, inside and out, the content contravening its own form, the doubt closer to being imagination than ever could have been thought possible. "I wait; asleep or awake, I wait" (ch. 46). At the end of *Lilith*, where both alternatives are plausible – sleeping or waking, trusting or doubting – nothing can be solved by thinking. MacDonald goes to the very verge that the theologians pulled short of. And there all that MacDonald's man can do is to wait between alternatives, to find what is true later and beyond – to see *what* comes after or *if* anything comes after at all, and how far either state is experienceable.

> He wants to know where he is, and where he ought to be and can be … It is a climbing and a striving to reach that point of vision where the multiplex crossings and apparent intertwisting of the lines of fact and feeling and duty shall manifest themselves as a regular and symmetrical design. (*A Dish of Orts*, p. 211)

It looks like a contradiction but at its most powerful, in its need and its pain and its seriousness, Victorian doubt is a commitment to the importance and the risk of belief. "There lives more faith in honest doubt, / Believe me," wrote Tennyson, "than in half the creeds" (*In Memoriam*, 96). Secularization is the great opportunity to re-find religion, or what religion stands for, not only despite the threat to faith but precisely because of it. In a Nazi concentration camp Dietrich Bonhoeffer wrote to Eberhard Nethge, July 16, 1944, that God's great challenge was for us to live "etsi deus non daretur" – as though God were not given.[18] That is the great secular experiment within reality.

3

Not So Straightforward: Realist Prose and What It Hides Within Itself

We think we know all about Victorian hypocrisy, when so-called "respectable" people tried to look so much better than they really were. But what about the person who tries to look as *bad* as he or she can?

Here, for example, is a man who plays the part of himself at his worst, presenting his most cynically indifferent self. With the help of alcohol, he plays it so well that he has almost forgotten that it *is* a part, and not the fate that it is also fast becoming. He is a lawyer who can do his real brain work only late at night after a binge, working virtually anonymously on behalf of a less talented but much more successful colleague whom he has known since school. Even in those youthful days he carried out the set exercises for the other boys but seldom did his own – as though he could only do the work part-time and in disguise, pretending that the talent he had for it wasn't related to himself. "You were always somewhere," he says to his old school-friend, "and I was always – nowhere":

> "And whose fault was that?"
> "Upon my soul, I am not sure that it was not yours. You were always driving and riving and shouldering and pressing to that restless degree that I had no chance for my life but in rust and repose."[1]

If he cannot bring himself to be a winner, there is just one other alternative left him. Beneath the assumed idleness, beneath the dissoluteness

54

that purges him of his proud, frustrated energy, it is only his despair of himself that can match his disgust at the world's competitiveness. This is a man you cannot know and you cannot explain. But there's a consistent behavioral pattern to his perverseness that, for shorthand, has become his "character."

In this story there is another figure who from the outside looks just like our man, as though they were identical twins. But in this second man, ours sees what he has fallen away from, recognizing in that other a version of what he himself could have been. For this twin or second self has won the heart of the woman whom our man loves, and she is the only person who could have made him want to live properly. Without her our man feels he is nothing. When his double is threatened with execution at the height of the French Revolution, what does our man do?

This wastrel-figure substitutes himself for his rival at the scaffold. He knows he can afford it; he has never lived; he isn't really a person, though he has that shape and form. The rival will go on to marry the woman he himself loves and raise a family both in place of him and yet also by his leave. And at the moment of execution, our man imagines the future he will have created by his death but will never see – a future wherein, he imagines, the woman will weep for him on the anniversary of this day, and her son will bear his name, turning it to better uses. His is not just a selflessly heroic act: it is also for the sake of the self he has thrown away in life. It is like turning self-destructiveness inside out into self-sacrifice instead. For the damned can only achieve in their crooked way what the saved seem to do more straightforwardly out of goodness. The lost souls must take themselves away from the salvation they leave behind, even by incorporating all that is bad within their own destruction.

A passive execution is transformed, disguisedly, into a last-minute action; a wasted nobody is turned into a scapegoat without anyone realizing it; a great redeeming generosity, unsustainable in day-to-day life, is achieved at death through the transmuted use of despair. He goes to the guillotine alongside a frightened young seamstress who at the last has seen through his disguise. Somehow the secret knowledge that he at least has *chosen* to be here helps her through her death, just as her shared knowing of the invisible truth helps him too. There are Victorian texts, mainly late ones, that relish the dramatic splitting of good and evil, as between Dr Jekyll and Mr Hyde. And even in the 1850s Dickens, the author of this particular story, loves the violent, veering swings from one extreme to another. But he uses the threat of the bad as the only way he knows of saving and renewing the good. And then eventually – establishing the classic mid-century Victorian way – he loves to hide the one thing *within* the other.

There is another example from Dickens to consider, from a quite different imagined world: this time it is a young woman who is disguised. Though you can guess easily enough, it is better not to use names: that way you can see the bare skeletal idea at work within the human form, rather than wrap it up within the themes of a too-well-known story. This young woman is probably a prostitute. Abused from an early age, she has lived all her life amidst a gang of child-thieves, under the tutelage of an aged dealer in partnership with the house-breaker who becomes her man. But when the gang abduct an orphaned middle-class boy and, in terrible parody of a family, begin to bring him up as she was brought up, then something in her – in part, the child she was, but partly also the mother she will never be – wants that boy out of it. Earlier she had got him back when he had run away, for fear lest he betray them; now, repentantly, she makes contact with the boy's guardians, in an effort to save him further damage within her under-world. From the moment she secretly plans the boy's rescue, she begins to live mentally (and almost madly) between two worlds, with the life she has habitually led as normal turned into a disguised cover for what is now within her mind. Instead of her usual ways, she now takes no notice of what is happening immediately around her or, rousing herself, joins in too forcibly, her mind "unable wholly to detach itself from old companions" and yet her thoughts "occupied with matters very different and distant from those in course of discussion by her companions."[2]

The immanent human thinking carried out by a realist novelist works like this: if the prostitute is no longer at home in one world because she is thinking of another, then suppose we take her through the looking glass, physically put her in the other respectable world, and then see what happens. It is like turning a thought round to its other side. Yet when this young woman *is* in the better, safer world of the middle classes, in negotiation with the boy's guardian, she still insists that she will not betray to the law the corrupt old man who has charge of the child-gang: "Bad life as he has led, I have led a bad life too; there are many of us who have kept the same course together, and I'll not turn upon them, who might – any of them – have turned upon me, but didn't, bad as they are."[3] It is the little words like "too" that do the work here. Or it is the way that the negative "but didn't" still stands for something, not only before the words "bad as they are" but effectively still after and despite them.

Such implicit loyalty, again not far from despair, is the right thing in the wrong place, a goodness-in-badness, like a misplaced heart doing its best for life in a degraded body. And it is to that wrong place that the fallen girl literally takes herself back, leaving the little boy safe in her stead behind her – even as a young lady who is her equivalent in that better world urges her to quit her old life, but in vain:

> "I am chained to my old life. I loathe and hate it now, but I cannot leave it. I must have gone too far to turn back, – and yet I don't know, for if you had spoken to me so, some time ago, I should have laughed it off. But," she said, looking hastily round, "this fear comes over me again. I must go home."
>
> "Home!" repeated the young lady, with great stress upon the word.
>
> "Home, lady," rejoined the girl.[4]

Back through the looking glass, it is "home," it is "family," it is a "life," simultaneously letting down *and* retaining all that those words should mean in terms of the great human types and templates. But the girl herself cannot finally be two people and cannot live in two worlds: someone else, more innocent, has to be her second self, her lost second chance. There may be something in her thoughts and her feelings that belongs to a different life but physically she remains in her present worse one. So the thinking has to go on in the space *between* herself and the boy she must save: it is almost an allegorical space here silently calling for salvation or redemption. And in all this there is such a rich and troubled mix of mind and body, mental and physical, self and other – as though, like some hybrid, human beings were either too much or too little for themselves, as they struggle for a place in the world. This is of course Dickens territory in the creation of that incongruous mixture, in the unlivable space between two worlds: "It involves the best and worst shades of our nature; much of its ugliest hues and something of its most beautiful; it is a contradiction, an anomaly, an apparent impossibility; but it is a truth."[5] That is what I mean by *human thinking* implicit or immanent within the Victorian novel: thinking not in terms of concepts but rather in respect of half-hidden stories, neglected people, and equivocal situations – and, more than that, thinking within an unnamed area in the emotional reservoir of life, sited in between the banks of definite conceptual categories, and saturated with too many overlapping human considerations to offer merely one simplified "idea" or abstracted "theme." That is what human beings are in this vision of life: experiments in what is too amorphous or contradictory for static reasoning, models of thinking out life in struggling practice.

In all this, Dickens's young woman stands for the double loyalty of Victorian fiction: loyal both to how it is in reality *and* to how else it might be in the really real nature of a world in better shape – a world often hidden and distorted within this one, confined inside people themselves too small to change very much. It is the rough obduracy and threatening determinism of the external social and economic changes, suddenly shocking and assaulting the Victorian world, that dramatize this sad dichotomy between within and without.

She looks like a prostitute but, as it is said of two coarsened, poor, and beaten mothers in another Dickens novel, "I think the best side of such people is almost hidden from us."[6] That is why in the face of such outcasts Dickens was, in his own way, also following something he recognized in the Gospels, in respect of the Christian capacity for surprising judgments amidst the lowly, or acts of grace in lieu of such judgment. For to Dickens, the class issue is no more and no less than the most dramatic example of what goes on in humans, trapped beneath outward circumstances and habitual hardenings. Too often what appears to be reality is a world in which there is a terrible barrier between self and others, between inside and out, restricting within the physical all that seems to reach and belong beyond it – while across that barrier there are, at another level, links in mind, emotion, and imagination that seem to deny the separation. It is like two wholly different world-views going on together. And what that makes for in Dickens are great changes of heart between the two views, even in small, half-comical cases.

For example: one of the lodgers in a house is a bailiff, a profession the rest of the lodgers detest on principle. But the man has lost his wife and is left with young children, so that even the grumpiest of the protesters relents against forcing him to give notice and quit the place: "Mr Gridley gave his consent gruff – but he gave it. He was always gruff with him, but he has been kind to the children since. A person is never known till a person is proved."[7] Principles, theories, ideas, clear distinctions, and separations: they are like thick fingers when what is required in human practice is a sort of fine micro-surgery, albeit administered by what are still rough and awkward practitioners. In the telegraphese of human thinking "he gave it gruff – but he gave it" is like the prostitute's "but didn't, bad as they are," only the other way round. The *syntax* in its twists and turns is finer than the *vocabulary* through which it is worked. That is to say: all that is achieved or resisted *through* the midst of the common human material entrenched within that predicament is a mark of the characters' very best, almost in spite of themselves.

So it is that Dickens loves it when low and limited people – often without the formally educated capacity for articulation – find themselves in near-limitless situations, having to make a little go a long way under pressure. For prose is *itself* for him a medium for immanent disguise – as though what might be called poetry can be hidden within the ongoing, lower medium of the ostensibly mundane.

Victorian fictional prose at first sight looks like the ordinary, common language of a new, expansive world of indiscriminate bulk and busy speed. It seems to go on and on in sheer mass accumulation without much in the way of form save narrative and description. It appears tied to linear time's peremptory successiveness, and as such is most apt for fictional serialization. But this prose is not as straightforward as it appears to be, line after line. Dickens in particular relishes concealing the high within the low, the serious within the comic, the transcendent within the common continuum — and then suddenly, momentarily, reveals the concealment with all the force of emotional recognition.

And just occasionally he will half show you the hidden tools of this trade in prose. For what it actually takes to form a human sentence, when the situation all around is severe and inhuman, is shown, almost in slow motion, in the following. Here, comically, the old servant-woman Peggotty struggles to speak big feelings breathlessly through the narrow keyhole to the little boy David. He has been shut in solitary confinement by his uncaring step-father, for all the weak protests of his scared mother, before he is to be sent away to boarding school:

> Then Peggotty fitted her mouth close to the keyhole, and delivered these words through it with as much feeling and earnestness as a key-hole has ever been the medium of communicating, I will venture to assert: shooting in each broken little sentence in a convulsive little burst of its own.
>
> "Davy, dear. If I ain't been azackly as intimate with you. Lately, as I used to be. It ain't because I don't love you. Just as well and more my pretty poppet. It's because I thought it better for you. And for someone else besides. Davy, my darling, are you listening? Can you hear?"
>
> "Ye-ye-ye-yes, Peggotty!" I sobbed.
>
> "My own!" said Peggotty, with infinite compassion. "What I want to say, is. That you must never forget me. For I'll never forget you. And I'll take as much care of your mama, Davy. As ever I took of you. And I won't leave her. The day may come when she'll be glad to lay her poor head. On Peggotty's arm again. And I'll write to you, my dear. Though I ain't no scholar. And I'll — I'll —" Peggotty fell to kissing the key-hole, as she couldn't kiss me. (*David Copperfield* (1850), ch. 4)

In that characteristic mixture of the ludicrous and the subtle, what Dickens offers here is a guide to appreciating all that makes for a sentence in Victorian fictional prose. Turn those "broken sentences" back into straightforward full ones and you will see how easy it is to miss the achievement involved in the act of their making. "What I want to say, is," for example, is itself a shorthand for the human intention, the emotional commitment, that usually lies undisclosed behind such utterances – as here, with Peggotty, they struggle to get across the threshold of inarticulacy to the needy boy: "Though I ain't no scholar." The phrases are like telegraphese. For the breathless, effortful pauses are almost like line-endings in poetry: "ain't been azackly as intimate with you / Lately, as I used to be" is a sensitive register of the painfully recognized shift from the baseline of the usual. In light of that difference, Peggotty knows that the true way to reassurance is no longer the simple positive – "I still love you" – but the double negative – "It *ain't* because I *don't* love you" – which acknowledges the terrible inference the child must have made, and imaginatively meets rather than simply denies it. *She doesn't love me,* he must have thought. But "Just as well and more" is the answer to "Lately, as I used to be." This almost synaptic connectiveness between phrases is what elsewhere in the novel is called "the mind of the heart." Thus, "What I want to say, is / That you must never forget me / For I'll never forget you." Again through the negatives, the woman gets the order of things exactly right. It is not even "I'll never forget you and you must never forget me," like some promised deal set out in reassuring sequence against the fear. Rather, the deeper positive suggestion here is that *at the very moment* you are remembering me, you will always know that I am remembering you. For the phrases are not really successive, they are simultaneous: *while* you think of me, you can be sure you are being thought of too. It is your never forgetting me – something in your power – that is the guarantee against loneliness here.

And now I want you to see Dickens doing the opposite in the same novel: gradually putting the broken little sentences back together again. Here the ostensibly simple young man Ham, betrayed by his fiancée Em'ly, tries somehow to find a language through which the far cleverer David may convey to her, on his behalf, that she has done Ham no harm. It isn't true, his life is in heart-broken pieces: but what goes on here is called "collecting himself":

We walked on, farther than we had walked yet, before he spoke again. He was not crying when he made the pauses I shall express by lines. He was merely collecting himself to speak very plainly.

61

"Merely"! This goes quietly "farther" than that, much "farther" than usual. The lines or dashes, like a notation for hearing and imagining, are implicitly there all the time in Victorian artistic punctuation; but for once they are here made visually explicit:

> "I loved her – and I love the mem'ry of her – too deep – to be able to lead her to believe of my own self as I'm a happy man. I could only be happy – by forgetting of her – and I'm afeerd I couldn't hardly bear as she should be told I done that. If you, being so full of learning, Mas'r Davy, could think of anything as might bring her to believe I wasn't greatly hurt: still loving of her, and mourning for her: anything as might bring her to believe as I was not tired of my life, and yet was hoping fur to see her without blame, where the wicked cease from troubling and the weary are at rest – anything as would ease her sorrowful mind, and yet not make her think as I could ever marry, or as 'twas possible that anyone could ever be to me what she was – I should ask of you to say that – with my prayers for her – that was so dear."
>
> I pressed his manly hand again, and told him I would charge myself to do this as well as I could. (*David Copperfield*, ch. 51)

It is at once the need to speak and the difficulty of speaking that make the words count. In the passage's great, long sentence there are *two* incompatible things offered almost at once: "Anything as might bring her to believe," *anything*, three times; always followed on the other side by "*still*" or by "*and yet*." Between all those "nots," it is an impossible combination – the deluding lie to save her from further guilt at his pain ("wasn't *greatly* hurt," "not tired of my *life*"); and yet the vulnerable truth to assure her of continuing fidelity ("not *make* her think as I could *ever* marry"). And paradoxically of course, both sides, though opposite, are born of the same love. A simple feeling trapped in a complex situation is what creates intelligence here. It is the intelligence that results from there being more than one thing to think about, more than one feeling to feel at a time. The sheer massed force of human content bursts the conventional forms in which it struggles for expression: the reader unexpectedly finds different *levels* of reality, different directions of thought, suddenly appearing along the same *line*.

It is like a development of that wonderful primal moment when children, learning to read from their prose primer, first find the sentence to be longer than one line on the page and go on over instead to another line without notice, stretching their thinking, making it a journey. Yet though Ham himself had seemed childish, low, and simple, not least of all to Em'ly herself, here he is genuinely "manly." For no one cleverer than Ham could put it better than Ham himself, as David himself well knows. It is like a death-bed speech that Ham also has to live on after. The situation is the wrong shape in the physical orientation of this world; its syntax can be given only negatively through mediation, on the page, via David. No one could say direct to Em'ly all that Ham wanted her both to hear and not to hear. That is where writing comes from – the failure of speaking; and that is why David, who can say little in reply to Ham and puts that little only in indirect reported speech, himself becomes a writer. For one simple thing Ham cannot do: let David tell her that this jilted man is unforgivingly angry with her, or that he cares nothing for her and will make himself happy again by forgetting her – even though that might be one way of letting Em'ly off that hook of knowing the lasting damage she has done him. It is as if to say: no truth without love; but no love without truth. It is the same with David at the death-bed of his childish young wife Dora when she says, speaking of herself in the past tense, that she sometimes thinks that she was not fit to be a wife: David does not simply lie ("You were a wonderful wife, Dora") or tell a cruel truth ("You're right, you were never mature enough") but says instead, in the syntax of the two of them in it together, "As fit as I to be a husband" (ch. 53). This again is the double loyalty of Victorian fiction, not transcending mundane difficulties but finding the good enclosed within them. Ham's "I should ask of you to say *that*," whatever *that* is, is a phrase that does in immediate retrospect all that "What I want to say, is" proposes in advance.

"That" – the word that *points* to something otherwise unnamable. It is like what William James said about forgetting a word or name: the empty space is left silently holding onto the potential of the idea by which it was once fulfilled. To the Victorian realists, "that" was what language was always doing, pointing to something real outside or beyond itself, which it was modeling and imagining. Hence Peggoty's effort to find the child David; hence Ham's effort to reach Em'ly. "Never forget" is the message from both of them, and it is the human subject-matter, often hidden within its most common and neglected forms, that Victorian realism works to represent, to recall and to save: art never for its own sake but for the sake of what, from outside art, art brings back within itself. "What I want to say, is," "I should ask of you to say that": if you can *see* the verbal effort, like this, at its bare minimum and in process of being forced into increasing complication, then you witness something akin to the fundamental essence and development of the human language-act – as if for the first time again. It isn't just in biology that the signs of evolution are revealed: for Herbert Spencer, in the development of complex sentences out of simple ones, in the development of Bach's counterpoint out of simple melody, there is the same branching law, the same underlying pattern – in all the divisions of human development.[8] In Ham's speech, there aren't just words; there is also the half-hidden language of the syntax itself, blindly feeling out the shape of the predicament from within: syntax is a mental tool responsive to need, in the shock of recognizing new human complexity. In that speech's implicit syntax, you can see the two urgent lines of thought going on in deep mental counterpoint – *anything* that can relieve her mind, *and yet* not make her think that I can forget her – in an almost musical notation of interwoven brain waves. The language of syntax is an instrument like a brain scanner employed in order to register the thought's insistent neurological pattern: as we trace the interrelated clauses, we see that *this* is what goes on *within* an ordinary person beset by extraordinary distress. And at the University of Liverpool we are currently working on using brain scanners to examine the inner neurological patterns and effects of such passages.[9] The aim is to use this heightened ordinary language and its syntax as a model of what human thinking is really like when it is forming itself, unprogrammed, in the midst of ongoing events.

★

By unprogrammed, I mean some change in shape, sensitive to what is unfolding, that emerges unplanned in the very midst of the prose's going along – even when the writing is about something you already think you know, something that has already happened, something not even fictional. I am thinking here of a moment in a great Victorian autobiography, where a writer transfers her novelist's skills to the writing of her own life. It is all long since past and safely in retrospect, it seems, and yet suddenly it becomes "real remembering." As another, later novelist puts it, real remembering is "if even for a flash, even a moment, being back in the experience itself. You remember pain with pain, love with love, one's real best self with one's best self."[10] Read the following from Mrs Oliphant, in memory of the dying of her mother, from her own posthumously published *Autobiography* (1899), and see where *you* think *real* remembering is registered most powerfully. At the time Mrs Oliphant was a married woman aged 26, with children of her own:

> She died in September 1854, suffering no attendance but mine, though she concealed from me how ill she was for a long time. I remember the first moment in which I had any real fear, speaking to the doctor with a sudden impulse, in the front of her door, all in a green shade with waving trees, demanding his real opinion. I do not think I had any understanding of the gravity of the circumstances. He shook his head, and I knew – the idea having never entered my mind before that she was to die. I recollect going away, walking home as in a dream, not able to go to her, to look at her, from whom I had never had a secret, with this secret in my soul that must be told least of all to her; and the sensation that here was something which would not lighten after a while as all my troubles had always done, and pass away. I had never come face to face with the inevitable before.[11]

There are longer sentences here and there are shorter ones. The longer ones in this memoir are generally narrative, factual, miming in their ongoing "ands" the woman's usual underlying assumption that everything would "lighten after a while as all my troubles had always done, and pass away." The shorter are like things stopped in their tracks, shocked by the dawning reality of the doctor's "*real* opinion": they are "never before" sentences ("the idea having never entered my mind before," "I had never come face to face … before"), new realizations that cannot be got over or easily gone on from. Interestingly, it is in the midst of the longest of the sentences that I think the most powerful example of "real remembering" suddenly occurs. For in the wandering sentence beginning "I recollect going away, walking home as in a dream " is lodged an extraordinary act of poetic syntax: "not able to go to her [from whom I had *never had a secret*] *with this secret*." Suddenly the sentence is no longer going linearly forward but oscillates back and forth between "never had a secret" and "with this secret," the two unbearably close together, like a shocking new boundary – of no more than a skin's width – created between daughter and mother. In fact we already know from the first sentence in this passage that the mother had long realized how close she was to death but hid it from the daughter ("she concealed from me how ill she was for a long time") – even as the daughter now feels she must hide it from the mother. And it is a further painful irony that the daughter now especially needs her mother – the person to whom she has naturally confided everything all her life – in order to bear the idea of the mother's own death. Yet though she tries to bear it alone, even her loyalty feels almost like a betrayal as well as a loneliness: it is her mother's thought – the thought of death – that the daughter is trying to have for her. Yet Mrs Oliphant feels she must protect her mother even from the needs of her own daughter, herself. It is like Esther in *Bleak House,* most aware of herself, in her illegitimacy, as her mother's dangerous secret. Or like Ham unable to say all he thinks of Em'ly, even (or especially) to Em'ly whom it most concerns. The reality is too much for the structures in which we hold it. For Mrs Oliphant is almost paradoxically unable "*to go to her*" or even "*to look at her*," given that the secret concerning *her* must now be told "*least of all*" to her. It is more like a notation than a description or narration: the reader can feel the repeated "her" lighting up different spots in the brain, forming new links in a strange new network of relations.

This is Mrs Oliphant's half-hidden genius within the ordinary. This is prose loyal to its subject-matter: ostensibly ordinary as it goes along and containing within it something larger or stranger than you had anticipated. There are levels hidden within the lines. You are not given ready-made themes or solid categories: they emerge only in fluid process. Thus, as a reader in the very midst of reading on and on, you have to make out what are unsignaled shifts and implicit contrasts in the free informality of linear prose – one thing passing into another by imperceptible gradations. It is as though you were having to read ordinary life itself, passing by with its meanings half-hidden and its questions already fading. "This *is* marriage," says David Copperfield's aunt to him when he complains of the un-ideal nature of his home. So here with Mrs Oliphant this is about the dying of a parent: a common theme we think we know all too well. But Mrs Oliphant is not bored with the subject-matter of apparently ordinary reality, does not to have to invent some stranger tragedy. The biggest shock would not be what is sensational – her mother turning out to be a murderer in some long-distant past. Nor need it be magical or fantastic. Rather, the biggest shock is that over the years, for all her love, Mrs Oliphant later finds that she cannot shut her eyes and fully describe her mother's face or analyze her character as though she were a separate person: "How little one realizes …" she says.[12] In realism, the greatest and most austere difference lies in finding out, amidst the reduced, normalized versions of itself, what, for example, *love* really means as in Henry James's "The Beast in the Jungle," or what *death* really means as in Tolstoy's "The Death of Ivan Ilyich." "The so-called magical realists …" complains the brain-surgeon protagonist of Ian McEwan's *Saturday* (2006), "What were these authors of reputation doing – grown men and women of the twentieth century – granting supernatural powers to their characters? … The supernatural was the recourse of an insufficient imagination, a dereliction of duty, a childish evasion of the difficulties and wonders of the real."[13]

The Victorian realists are scared of taking life for granted, of living by firelight within Plato's cave and not seeing the sun outside, or, as George Eliot puts it in *Middlemarch*, of walking round well wadded with stupidity. There's another male character in Dickens, first presented as all too anonymous a type, who realizes he has never intervened on behalf of a wronged work-colleague. For years that colleague has had to carry on living down a bad reputation for past irregularity, even though by never forgetting it himself he had become an altered man.

But, institutionalized within the business, no one had recognized the humble change, let alone protested against the injustice still meted out despite it:

> "We go on in our clockwork routine, from day to day, and can't make out, or follow, these changes. They – they're a metaphysical sort of thing. We – we haven't leisure for it. We – we haven't courage. They're not taught at schools or colleges, and we don't know how to set about it. In short we are so d—d business-like," said the gentleman, walking to the window, and back, and sitting down again, in a state of extreme dissatisfaction and vexation.
>
> "I am sure," said the gentleman, rubbing his forehead again; and drumming on the table as before, "I have good reason to believe that a jog-trot life, the same from day to day, would reconcile one to any-thing. One don't see anything, one don't hear anything, one don't know anything; that's the fact. We go on taking everything for granted, and so we go on, until whatever we do, good, bad, or indifferent, we do from habit. Habit is all I shall have to report, when I am called on to plead to my conscience on my death-bed. 'Habit,' says I; 'I was deaf, dumb, blind, and paralytic, to a million things, from habit.' 'Very business-like indeed, Mr What's-your-name,' says Conscience, "but it won't do here!'" (*Dombey and Son* (1848), ch. 33)

"They – they' re … We – we haven't": that first paragraph reads like the halted stutter of a belatedly new language, looking back on the familiar, as from the death-bed, with a finally awakened point of view. Otherwise for the most part we just go on and on sinking into famil-iar patterns and ongoing ways that, without a stopping-place, can get us used to almost anything. What the realists look for is the jolt in the brain that William James describes when the real meaning of a repeated act suddenly lights up the mind. They seek that point at which the sheer accumulation of complicated human *content* begins to be too much for the habitual, conventional, and institutional *forms* in which it is contained.

It is like that inexhaustible fullness that Ruskin describes in a sky painted by Turner – when the eye can't rest on one cloud without being drawn to the next and "lost over and over again in every wreath";

when "there is not one line out of the millions there which repeats another, not one which is unconnected with another, not one which does not in itself convey histories of distance and space, and suggest new and changeful form." Then, says Ruskin, we know that we are in the presence of something too rich and dense and varied for the human mind to be able merely to invent or control:

> though these forms are too mysterious and too delicate for us to ana-lyze, though all is so crowded and so connected that it is impossible to test any single part by particular laws, yet ... we may be sure that this infinity can only be based on truth, that it *must* be nature, because man could not have originated it, and that every form must be faithful, because none is like another. (*Modern Painters*, vol. 1 (1843), part 2, sec. 3, ch. 3, para. 24)

Writers likewise know when, after much work, they have put them-selves into a place, or found a mood, or created a situation, in which thoughts seem to come thick and fast, from various different direc-tions, unpredictably and together. Then they have made something that goes beyond themselves. In a novel this most often occurs when, in the middle of the book, several parts come together to form more than the sum of themselves – as though the very life of the book were taking over, arising out of the bursting and interconnecting contents of the work. One of our recent MA students, Fiona Jones, cited to me a little while ago an equivalent infinity in an emotionally saturated solution created within Dickens's *Bleak House*, where suddenly almost the whole novel seems to come together in immediate memory.

It is this. An old housekeeper is the mother of two sons, one suc-cessful, the other a long-time runaway turned soldier. Attended by Mrs Bagnet, another matriarchal figure in the book, who silently wit-nesses what is happening, Mrs Rouncewell at last finds her lost son, albeit under false accusation in prison:

> George, who is writing at his table, supposing himself to be alone does not raise his eyes, but remains absorbed. The old housekeeper looks at him, and those wandering hands of hers are quite enough for Mrs Bagnet's confirmation ...

Not a rustle of the housekeeper's dress, not a gesture, not a word, betrays her. She stands looking at him as he writes on, all unconscious, and only her fluttering hands give utterance to her emotions. But they are very eloquent; very, very eloquent. Mrs Bagnet understands them. They speak of gratitude, of joy, of grief, of hope; of inextinguishable affection, cherished with no return since this stalwart man was a stripling; of a better son loved less, and this son loved so fondly and so proudly; and they speak in such touching language, that Mrs Bagnet's eyes brim up with tears, and they run glistening down her sun-browned face.

"George Rouncewell! O my dear child, turn and look at me!"

The trooper starts up, clasps his mother round the neck, and falls down on his knees before her. Whether in a late repentance, whether in the first association that comes back upon him, he puts his hands together as a child does when it says its prayers, and raising them towards her breast, bows down his head, and cries. (*Bleak House* (1853), ch. 55)

It is important that while George supposes himself alone, all unconscious, he is being tenderly watched from a now brief distance. It is important that the language that Mrs Bagnet can read in the mother's fluttering hands precedes the outburst of any finite spoken words. It is important that Mrs Bagnet, equivalent mother, is a silent witness, helping to hold the mounting resonance of the thing in its slow motion. For this is not the mere sentimentality that a hasty postmodern reader might label it to be. This is the establishment of a prior ground — prior to speech, prior to reunion — in which everything for a moment is held in brimming solution. It is like the DNA, the great genetic pool of the parent–child relationship, the human story's template that is full of everything possible in life's twists and turns. Not one line, said Ruskin of Turner, does not convey "histories of distance and space." Thus lodged here is not only the whole emotional span of joy, grief, and hope all at once — "of inextinguishable affection, cherished with no return" — but also the temporal span of a whole life, man and boy, that rushes into the compressed space between "late repentance" and "first association." Nor could any one have predicted that wonderful, almost unfairly emergent little touch of sheer life, when the other brother is compared in passing with this prodigal son: "a better son loved less."

But then Dickens returns to silence in a wonderfully constructed sentence. "She can ask, and he can answer, nothing connected for a time." And yet when George can begin to explain, it is as though there is a change from something large in the prior human silence of emotional life to something small and narrowed and rigidified – to a story that has diminished almost to a non-story, as time passed. When he first ran away, George tells his mother, he made believe that he cared for nobody and nobody cared for him. Later he did not write because by then it seemed too late to make contact, and it was almost better for him to be dead to her:

> "There was I, a dragoon, roving, unsettled, not self-made like [my brother] but self-unmade – all my earlier advantages thrown away, all my little learning unlearnt, nothing picked up but what unfitted me for most things that I could think of. What business had I to make myself known? After letting all that time go by me, what good could come of it? The worst was past with you, mother. I knew by that time (being a man) how you had mourned for me, and wept for me, and prayed for me; and the pain was over, or was softened down, and I was better in your mind as it was."
>
> The old lady sorrowfully shakes her head; and taking one of his powerful hands, lays it lovingly upon her shoulder.
>
> "No, I don't say that it was so, mother, but that I made it out to be so."

This "made it out to be so," like the earlier making believe that no one cares, puts into words what he has long been trying to do with that dwelling-place where thoughts live and grow, in connection with the primary, instinctive belief of love. While he was diminishing and denying those thoughts, she was holding onto what remains a sort of emotional birthright for humans in Dickens – a life's birthright too often withheld at first or wasted at last. But that is the underlying source-place or human reservoir that Dickens often emotionally opens out again in his novels, in defiance of its attenuation into the dwindling, linear narrative of lost possibilities. We can hardly make out such changes: they are a metaphysical sort of thing. But Victorian realists do not want to transcend the physical, they want to show the metaphysical arising even from within it.

That is why the art of realist prose is the best model of how, as we go on and go on horizontally, there is still in the midst of the ongoing something that belongs to a different dimension too often neglected or left behind.[14] I have been doing work with a PhD research student, Melissa Raines, examining the manuscripts of Victorian novels. Amidst the immediate thought-processes and subsequent amendments of the great Victorian novelists, we went in search of the hidden, pre-publication equivalent of those informal dashes and almost musical notations we have seen in those Peggotty and Ham passages. For the handwritten manuscripts are often more free and flowing, even in their punctuation markings, than is registered in the finally rather heavy house-style that the publishers required. Here are two simple, tiny, but telling examples from George Eliot, both of them to do with moments on the verge of that metaphysical inner change that Dickens's man rightly claims are not taught sufficiently in schools and colleges.

Example one. Maggie Tulliver is a passionately impetuous character who, as she stumbles along amidst the jolts of her life, is agonizingly aware of the mistakes she has made the very moment *after* she has made them. Here, even as a child, she finds herself suddenly grieving over her impulsive cutting of her own hair:

> She could see clearly enough, now the thing was done, that it was very foolish, and that she should have to hear and think more about her hair than ever; for Maggie rushed to her deeds with passionate impulse, and then saw not only their consequences, but what would have happened if they had not been done, with all the detail and exaggerated circumstance of an active imagination. (*The Mill on the Floss* (1860), ch. 7)

In the manuscript (also used by the novelist A. S. Byatt in her excellent Penguin edition) what George Eliot wrote, in the free flow of her hand, was: "She could see clearly enough now the thing was done that it was very foolish" – no comma after "enough"; no comma after "done." The text goes on forward just as Maggie "rushed to her deeds," the consequences and alternatives realized too late with just as much excited exaggeration as had caused her to ignore them in the first place. In the inner feel of the shaping of the passage, "now the thing was done" is for George Eliot not so much a sectioned-off stage of formal realization but a temporal irony caught by an unsynchronized girl in the midst of immediate retrospection. There are so many clauses existing in a George Eliot sentence – and for much the same reason as there are so many characters in *Middlemarch*: each clause, as either further consequence or lost alternative, represents a thought seeking actualization of itself in a life, as a distinctly shaped character with a story. If they could only stop, get out of the sentence in which they are subordinate, take a new direction of their own, be revised into a new paragraph! Then they would be like human seeds of possibility growing into fully released realization on their own. But there is not always time or room or sufficient amplitude of thought for them to do so. John Stuart Mill, writing in his essay on Bentham,[15] was very aware of what could be omitted even by the very act of formulation, when a thinker did not create sufficient mental space to rescue a momentarily occurring thought from its syntactic subordination. A mental framework and context could leave out as much as it let in. A thought might have no home for itself, in which to be realized.

This is not so with David Copperfield: in his honesty and his insecurity alike, he will let in any thought, which is one reason why the novel has to be so ample. Even after Steerforth has betrayed the Peggotty family by seducing Little Em'ly, David cannot help immediately recalling all that had been good in the man he had loved since schooldays. If I had met Steerforth again face to face, says David, I would have been as weak as the child I had been when idolizing him at boarding school. But then the sentence suddenly changes direction: "as weak as a spirit-wounded child, in all but the entertainment of a thought that we could ever be re-united." And then he gives that change of direction its own sentence: "That thought I never had" (ch. 32). For Steerforth is dead to him. David can bear to think of all the thoughts he had and all the thoughts he could no longer have.

But Bentham was a formal philosopher who never knew *what* he didn't know, or *that* he didn't know: he had, said Mill, all the completeness of limited men.

For George Eliot, however, all the possible thoughts and all the potential characters are part of one ever-ongoing whole, one world, one great complex sentence if any mortal could ever write it. Thus in the clauses of just a single life: Maggie, it is written, rushed into actions, "*then* saw *not only* their consequences, but what *would* have happened if they had *not* been done." What the sentence shows is what George Eliot elsewhere says: "Character too is a process and an unfolding" (*Middlemarch*, ch. 15). But in that fluid *process* that hardens as we go along, characters can finally live only one life: the thoughts they cannot bear, the lives they will not lead are like clauses within a main sentence that goes on without or despite them. And if these passing possibilities can find no other embodiment, they become "George Eliot" in those novels of hers, as though she were the race's memory of unrealized human potential, seeking to hold together life itself as though in one great complex sentence. "He knew how he felt," it is said of the protagonist in Henry James's "The Beast in the Jungle," "but, besides knowing that, she knew how he looked as well" – the woman who is the protagonist's neglected companion

> had achieved, by an art indescribable, the feat of at once – or perhaps it was only alternately – meeting the eyes from in front and mingling her own vision, as from over his shoulder, with their peep through the apertures.

So it is with George Eliot as companion to her own characters.

Here is a second example of the uses of manuscript from *Middlemarch* itself, again to do with what is half hidden amidst ongoing fluidity. Here a young woman, like an older Maggie, on honeymoon in Rome, finds herself overwhelmed. She does not yet know, as the reader does, that she has chosen the wrong man. It is not tragic or unusual, says George Eliot, for a young woman to cry six weeks after her wedding when she finds a new real future replacing the virginally imaginary one:

Dorothea was crying, and if she had been required to state the cause, she could only have done so in some such general words as I have already used: to have been driven to be more particular would have been like trying to give a history of the lights and shadows; for that new real future which was replacing the imaginary drew its material from the endless minutiæ by which her view of Mr Causabon and her wifely relation, now that she was married to him, was gradually changing with the secret motion of a watch-hand from what it had been in her maiden dream. It was too early yet for her fully to recognize or at least admit the change, still more for her to have readjusted the devotedness which was so necessary a part of her mental life that she was almost sure sooner or later to recover it. (*Middlemarch* (1871–2), ch. 20)

It should come as no surprise that, again, the commas inserted around the clause "now that she was married to him" in the published version were not present in the original manuscript. It would be too steady for Dorothea to mark it off; she is still in the midst of its discovery, just behind the beat: "It was too early yet for her to fully to recognize or at least admit the change." The levels shift, unsignaled, within the line – "too early yet" played off against "fully"; "recognize" played off against "admit" via "at least": as you are in process of going along, you only realize the mental change just after it has happened. This woman is in the midst of such change, without a sense of form or orientation any more. The "endless minutiæ" of content at the subliminal level of the Victorian novel will gradually mass to create the conscious message: *this is marriage*. What fascinates George Eliot is the moment that T. S. Kuhn in *The Structure of Scientific Revolutions* (1962) was to describe as a paradigm shift, the point at which an old framework of understanding becomes so shaken by realized anomalies within itself that it must give way to a successor. But it is that strange place *in between* one damaged paradigm and its unknown future replacement that is most crucial to George Eliot, in the psychological subconscious equivalent of "the secret motion of a watch-hand." It is that holding-place that her novels make for, in their brimming content. *Middlemarch*, said William James, was "fuller of human stuff than any novel that was ever written."[16]

Clearly George Eliot did not mind the clarifying house-style set up by the printers, and collaborated in using it in her final versions. She must have believed that the text's underlying nervous system would still, in its rhythm, come through the public appearance of the text. That published text can act like a palimpsest, the earlier template still felt behind the finalized public version of itself. Melissa Raines's argument is that what goes on here is like what happens all over the place in George Eliot when you attentively *read* into the life within the novels. That is to say: on the outside you think you see a solid and formidable woman, for example, but underneath there are hidden traces of something different at the subterranean level of the brain-nerves:

> If she had only been more haggard and less majestic, those who had glimpses of her outward life might have said she was a tyrannical, griping harridan, with a tongue like a razor. No one said exactly that; but they never said anything like the full truth about her, or divined what was hidden under that outward life – a woman's keen sensibility and dread, which lay screened behind all her petty habits and narrow notions, as some quivering thing with eyes and throbbing heart may lie crouching behind withered rubbish. (*Felix Holt* (1866), ch. 1)

That is what the manuscript text is, within and beneath its own finished appearance: a thin-skinned nervous organism, painfully sensitive to whatever touches it. It carries within it those secret inner quiverings, at both neural and draft level, which George Eliot's friend and contemporary Herbert Spencer described in *The Principles of Psychology* as the tiny nervous blows of thought:

> The state of consciousness so generated is, in fact, comparable in quality to the initial state of consciousness caused by a blow (distinguishing it from the pain or other feeling that commences the instant after); which state of consciousness, caused by a blow, may be taken as the primitive and typical form of nervous shock.[17]

These grammatical blows or shocks are the difficult places where the reader and the character are being challenged by nerve-like thoughts of a painful, instinctive, almost pre-conscious nature. If we had a keen vision and feeling of all *ordinary* human life, says George Eliot in the great paragraph preceding the account of Dorothea's tears, "it would be like hearing the grass grow, and the squirrel's heart beat, and we should die of that roar which lies on the other side of silence" (*Middlemarch*, ch. 20). We don't see anything, we don't hear anything, we don't know anything, says Dickens's man. But great writing here means seeking to reach the dulled brain even in the midst of what it assumes to be not unusual, simply habitual. It makes you hear the grass grow.

The great listener to these near-silent inner murmurs, pitched well below the normal level of human hearing, is George Eliot herself. Watch your own words, she says in *The Mill on the Floss*, which also came to mean read your own writing even in the midst of forming it. It is as though she finds herself, in the second place as "George Eliot," in the midst of what she herself has created in the first, caught now in between her own separated couples, registering all that they do not say to each other. Thus the eager, youthful Dorothea and the aging failed scholar Casaubon, as she urges him on to the never-to-be-completed work he is always subconsciously hiding from: "'All those rows of volumes,' she said, looking at his significantly endless array of research notes, 'Will you not make up your mind what part of them you will use, and begin to write the book which will make your vast knowledge useful to the world?'"

The excessive feeling manifested would alone have been highly disturbing to Mr Casaubon, but there were other reasons why Dorothea's words were among the most cutting and irritating to him that she could have been impelled to use. She was as blind to his inward troubles as he to hers; she had not yet learned those hidden conflicts in her husband which claim our pity. She had not yet listened patiently to his heart-beats, but only felt that her own were beating violently. In Mr Casaubon's ear, Dorothea's voice gave loud emphatic iteration to those muffled suggestions of consciousness which it was possible to explain as mere fancy, the illusion of exaggerated sensitiveness: always when such suggestions are unmistakably repeated from without, they are resisted as cruel and unjust. We are angered even by the full acceptance of our humiliating confessions – how much more by hearing in hard

distinct syllables from the lips of a near observer, those confused murmurs which we try to call morbid, and strive against as if they were the
oncoming of numbness! And this cruel outward accuser was there in
the shape of a wife – nay, of a young bride. (*Middlemarch*, ch. 20)

He wanted a young bride who would be uncritical – even at the very
moment that she herself didn't know she *wasn't* being. Able to hold in
her head more than one thought at a time, able to be more than one
person at a time, "George Eliot" is triggered into being by a bursting
syntax, by all that Dorothea is repeatedly "not yet" able to be: "*she* was
as blind to *his* inward troubles as *he* to *hers*." Although I have italicized
the pronouns to make manifest the tremendous turn of the novelist's
mind from one side to another, it is the paradoxical syntax of "as …
as" that is really the underlying brain restructurer. There are always
these signs that George Eliot works hard for in her manuscripts –
sometimes existent in space, as here between two people; sometimes
in time, as in the phrases "not yet" or "now that"; but almost invariably
registered in quiet, tiny, often single-word parentheses inserted in the
midst of both situation and sentence. Thus George Eliot first wrote
simply "she had not yet learned his hidden conflicts," then in the
manuscript crossed out "his" and replaced it with "those" – that pointing word then opening up the sentence so that she could now write
"those hidden conflicts in her husband" and add "which deserve our
pity," thereafter further amending "deserve" to "claim" as though she
could almost hear those conflicts from the other side of silence unconsciously calling for a help the man himself could not bear to want or
to receive. Later, Casaubon is as frightened of Dorothea's pity as he is
here of her unwitting criticism: both contain the judgment upon
himself he is seeking to suppress.

Realism says: think of Casaubon as though he were a real person –
he doesn't know he is unconsciously confessing his secret thoughts to
George Eliot, for George Eliot is of course not there to him. If he did
know it, it would be far worse to him than anything even Dorothea
had said. Such realism is not naive but just as inventive as any modern
meta-fictional play, only less concerned with showing its own clever-
ness: phrases such as "*those* hidden conflicts which claim *our* pity"

implicitly point *you*, the reader, to imagine what it would be like if your innermost thoughts, disguised even from yourself, were over-heard by some real-life equivalent to George Eliot (such as God used to be). The novel as a form is *that* ambitious in its reach and its claims. It not only seeks to turn inside and out between Dorothea and Casaubon; it seeks to turn itself inside out, toward its readers and the life outside of which it offers its version within.

At any rate, in aiming to situate itself *between* literature and life, the realist novel finds its greatest go-between in George Eliot herself. At first, George Eliot is no more than a level of consciousness cre-ated by the capacity to write a sentence such as "She was as blind to his inward troubles as he to hers," making for a third presence emer-gent by the act of writing above and between the two others. But George Eliot is never content to leave "as ... as" a mere enabling micro-structure, a technical tool of artistic syntax: always she wants to translate what it means to be able to produce such evolved struc-tures; she wants to translate them out of art, out of specialist language, out of hiding, out of transience, into solid macro-terms, into the emotional human attitude in real life that the technical capacity stands for. George Eliot is thus – in all that she can superhumanly create, accept, judge, forgive – just as much a character in the book, in the very act of writing it, as any of the Middlemarch people around her.

But she also knows that she herself would not do much better than her Casaubons or Dorotheas were she no more than a charac-ter back in real life again, without the advantage of authorship. At the end of *Adam Bede* (1859), Adam himself has reached a posi-tion very close to George Eliot's own in terms of learning compas-sion. Hetty had left him, had gone after the young squire who had made her pregnant – that Arthur whom Adam had considered his friend as well as his patron – and in desperation had left her new-born child to die in the fields. That Adam, like a deeper version of Dickens's Ham, has suffered not only because of Hetty but also for the sake of Hetty, and is even through sympathetic pain a better man for that, makes George Eliot think two things almost at once in chapter 54. One is that it is not ignoble to feel that the fuller life which a sad experience has brought us is worth our own personal share of pain: surely it is not possible to feel otherwise, any more than it would be possible for a man with a cataract to regret the painful process by which his dim blurred sight of men as trees walking had been exchanged for clear outline and effulgent day.

The other, that a softened Adam, who finds comfort in Dinah

could never thank God for another's misery. And if I were capable of that narrow-sighted joy in Adam's behalf, I would still know he was not the man to feel it for himself: he would have shaken his head at such a sentiment, and said, "Evil's evil, and sorrow's sorrow, and you can't alter its nature by wrapping it up in other words. Other folk were not created for my sake, that I should think all square when things turn out well for me."

Whatever the effect on Adam, Hetty is Hetty, deported and broken, still. For all the interconnections in feeling, registered microscopically in the fluid draft forms of the manuscript, there are still, finally, in realism terrible and unbridgeable separations at the sheer physical level. This is the hardness in the wiring we saw in the first chapter of this book.

No one can be George Eliot; Marian Evans herself could hardly become her. "I at least have so much to do in unravelling certain human lots and seeing how they were woven and interwoven," she writes in the midst of *Middlemarch*, "that all the light I can command must be concentrated on this particular web" (ch. 15). This "I" is not merely the voice of "the narrator" as we call it all too technically. It is as much struggling as omniscient. And above all it is a person admitting its own human reality, sharing with readers the underlying real purpose, in the midst of trying to write fiction that is as close to life as possible. For George Eliot, as far as possible in her superhuman honesty, nothing is to be hidden finally – nothing hidden away within art; nothing neglected within life. "If there isn't a God," the novelist Stanley Middleton once said to me whilst he was still my teacher, "then George Eliot will do."[18]

4

A Literature In Time

Prose Ways

In a letter of March 1, 1860, Elizabeth Gaskell reported that she was reading Trollope's *Framley Parsonage* in 16 monthly installments and wished that the long novel would go on for ever. It seemed to her almost the same as being absorbed in living time itself.

There were no sensational cliff-hangers at the end of each serial part, or if there were, expectations were defeated by the subsequent inconclusiveness of events. By the end of the fifth installment, chapter 15, for example, the clergyman Mark Robarts has been warned by his austere older colleague, Mr Crawley, against his looming descent into worldly extravagance and consequent money-troubles, and the elder leaves the young man almost in tears. It ought to be a decisive, life-changing moment in which the young man finally rises above what has been going on for far too long. In fact, when we meet Mark Robarts again, reappearing four chapters later at the beginning of the seventh installment, he has been compromised into purchasing another horse in the meantime, as if through the interlayering of the novel his life went on even while not written about. For although he had at first "made up his mind" to face his unscrupulous creditors, "then again, he unmade it" when he thought of the poverty and ridicule he would encounter as a result. But, as with so much else in the lapse of time, it is not that he is simply oblivious of the warning Crawley furnished: "he was not oblivious of it. He was even mindful of it; but mindful of it in such a manner that his thoughts on the subject were now-a-days always painful" (ch. 14). The thought of what he is doing does not become consolidated into mind, or resolved into character, but goes back down to being no more than an uneasy part of what he continues to do, untransformed. In principle, Trollope says, "a man always can do right, even though he has done wrong before" (ch. 12): but of course the gradually cumulative effect of getting used to the wrong, unthinkingly making it a part of one's ordinary life without a crisis to make it stop, renders it ever harder to turn back.

That serial gradualness, without a dramatic moment in its happening, is Trollope's forte, as it is that of Mrs Gaskell herself, especially in *Wives and Daughters*, or that of Mrs Oliphant. Yet in its sense of people letting themselves go along with things, it is not cynical as so often and so wittily in Thackeray. The difference between Thackeray and Trollope is what is at stake in a single sentence from Mrs Oliphant's own *Hester* (1883): "Human nature may be easy to see through, but it is very hard to understand" (ch. 17). For Trollope's great realist thought is this: that, for better *and* worse, human beings can go on with their lives, almost regardless of something terribly important within them, yet also without whatever that is ever really going away. But it is not even a thought as such, indeed precisely is not one. For as Mrs Gaskell writes in a letter, March 15, 1859, on the art of the novelist:

> I think you must observe what is *out* of you, instead of examining what is *in* you. It is always an unhealthy sign when we are too conscious of any of the physical processes that go on within us; & I believe in like manner that we ought not to be too cognizant of our mental proceedings, only taking note of the results. But certainly – whether introspection be morbid or not – it is not a safe training for a novelist. It is a weakening of the art which has crept in of late years.[1]

For this sort of novelist, different from George Eliot, thinking should go on implicitly *inside* the life and action of the novel instead of inside a self or a commentator. That is why R. H. Hutton spoke of Trollope as ostensibly a spectator to his own novels, "a man who has minutely watched the *succession* of events."[2] His novel-thinking is like the following, to take a simple example from *The Last Chronicle of Barset* (1867). Grace Crawley is daughter of the clergyman who gave Mark Robarts his warning in *Framley Parsonage* (1861); only, with bitter irony, Crawley himself is now under shameful suspicion of stealing a check. Trollope has Grace find refuge with Mrs Dale and her bravely saddened daughter, Lilly, who was badly jilted by an adventurer in *The Small House at Allington* (1864). There is one little but rich moment in chapter 28 of *The Last Chronicle*, after Major Grantly has suddenly and nobly talked to Mrs Dale of courting Grace in spite of all the scandal surrounding her: Trollope has Lilly's mother reflect thus: "Mrs Dale when she was left alone could not but compare the good fortune which was awaiting Grace, with the evil fortune which had fallen on her child ... she almost envied Grace Crawley her lover." Trollope has set up the story of Grace alongside the story of Lilly, and brought them together implicitly in their persons – and *then*, fluidly shifting level, Trollope has a third person in Mrs Dale embody the passing thought of that comparison, while also struggling to be fair within the limits of her own inevitably partial point of view ("*almost* envied"). The novelist makes these different things happen at once in the converging and diverging of the novel's various lines, but says nothing explicitly. It is, as Mrs Oliphant said in a review of the novel, characteristically "a mingled simplicity and subtlety."[3]

It could be sensational stuff. Twenty years before the novel begins, Lady Mason in Trollope's *Orley Farm* (1862) had desperately forged a codicil to the will of her late, aged husband, so that the estate should pass to their new baby son and not to the already wealthy children of the old man's first marriage. But it is not the forgery, or even the plot of its discovery, that interests Trollope so much as how she lived with it afterward – and how she has now to live with the possibility of being found out so long after. "What if after twenty years of tranquillity all her troubles must now be recommenced?" she asks herself in the novelist's use of free indirect discourse, fading in and out between narrator and character in ways that suit Trollope's love of what is barely thought, "Why was it that she was so much greater a coward now than she had been?" (ch. 12). It is the casual unimportance of the momentary act, or her making it unimportant over so many years, that is paradoxically the most significant aspect of this frighteningly austere vision. "It was matter of wonder to her now, as she looked back at her past life, that her guilt had sat so lightly on her shoulders" (ch. 53). Time here is not a background to story, is not sacrificed to the driving rhythm of sensational plot, but is itself an essential element in the nature of the experience, in what it means to live with and in a situation. This chapter is to do with that Victorian discovery of living defeasibly in time.

Defeasibility means the liability to annulment and re-evaluation in light of subsequent change or the occurrence of extra factors. I take the term from the philosopher Anthony Kenny in his *Will, Freedom and Power* (1975). There Kenny compares the formal logic of the classical three-stage syllogism taking a thinker securely from valid premise to satisfactory conclusion – "All men are mortal. Socrates is a man. Socrates is mortal" – with the much looser procedures of practical thinking, as in this simple little example:

I'm to be in London at 4.15

If I catch the 2.30 I'll be in London at 4.15

So I'll catch the 2.30

Kenny points out that there is a further unstated premise there, namely that I don't want to be in London any earlier than I have to be. But the logic is defeasible because the conclusion is vulnerable to the addition of further premises or considerations around or before the initial one. Perhaps, for instance, the 2.30 is always crowded to bursting point and it would be a good thing to work on the train, in which case I may take an earlier, less busy train.[4] Practical thinking is not self-enclosed in the way that formal logic is, but in its potential proliferation has both the freedom and the uncertainty of being open to life. That looseness, the branching out of further and further considerations along the way, *is* the realist novel in all the ostensible untidiness and contingency of human praxis. Of course there are always in Trollope rather dodgy young men who take risks with the company they keep or the courses they adopt, hoping to get away it; but what one of them says in *The Duke's Children* (1880) is deeper than the motives of its sayer: "It's just like anything else, if nothing comes of it then it's all right" (ch. 66). It may not be all right, morally, but there is a serious and rather ordinarily mysterious sense in which life in the present is constantly in thrall to its ever-ongoing outcomes and is continually reshaped, too late, by what contingently it leads to.

The novel-form is part of the story of the nineteenth-century reformation of human thinking: the minute gradualism of change disclosed by Lyell's geological studies in his opposition to theories of seismic catastrophe; the process philosophy inherent in Darwin's account of biological evolution; the shift from ever-fixed categories, types, and species to change and chance and flux over unimaginably long periods of time. As early as the 1840s John Stuart Mill had argued against the truth-value of syllogistic logic in so far as there were no universal truths, no absolute generalizations that could stand as unshakeable premises from which to deduce irrefutable consequences: all was a matter of induction, of the gathering of scientific particulars to serve as predictive laws.

But Trollope, neither logician nor scientist, never thought of himself as clever. And that was his advantage as a novelist. He was a poor boy bullied at public school, made to feel large and stupid and slow and awkward, and three times failed to win a scholarship to Oxbridge. The disgrace of his schooldays, he wrote in his *Autobiography* (1883), clung to him for the rest of his life. He had to play the long game and he played it for the rest of his life. By the time he came to the writing of novels – long novels, including two extended series, the Barsetshire and Palliser chronicles, each of six volumes – his activity had become in the words of Henry James "a huge serial."[5] And in it what Trollope was especially good at was not allowing ideas to take over, either in himself or in his characters, as though they were the controlling force in human beings: rather, with an almost physical intelligence, he invisibly excelled in letting things go along in time, letting things slowly build up, to happen or to fail to happen. It was as though time did the thinking and the probing.

Often, character in Trollope is not only defended but almost defined by various versions of obstinacy, as human beings try to resist the thoughts and possibilities that time offers. So it is with Grace Crawley sadly rejecting the suit of Major Grantly, because of being in the midst of her father's still unresolved trial:

> "I feel we are all disgraced, and that I will not take disgrace into another family."
> "Grace, do you love me?"
> "I love no one now, – that is, as you mean. I can love no one. I have no room for any feeling except for my father and mother." (*The Last Chronicle of Barset*, ch. 30)

For Crawley himself the whole novel is an extended continuous "now," himself stranded in prolonged suspense between a past he cannot remember and the looming court-trial that will investigate it. One sentence, making a paragraph at a chapter end, serves as a momentarily frozen "still" of the man marooned:

> "And am I a thief?" he said to himself, standing in the middle of the road, with his hands up to his forehead. (ch. 13).

The tense is essentially present, the conjunction typically "and," the adjective characteristically "middle." But as Grace says, the key word is commonly "now" in Trollope – the sheer succession of "nows" moving on through, or despite, or around the characters.

Every year, Johnny Eames stubbornly promises himself that he will propose to Lilly Dale, hoping she has finally got over her feckless first lover. "If now you are ready for me, then, Lilly, am I, as ever, still ready for you." He will say "if now" again and again every year "as ever," he tells himself, already feeling like an old man, then remembering that he is only 27 and she 24 (*The Last Chronicle of Barset*, ch. 35). It is characteristic of this novel that Johnny Eames should be proud of his constancy to Lilly and yet "in some sort, he was also ashamed of it" (ch. 15). And as a way of keeping going, there is even a part of Johnny willing to flirt on the side with other women. It is also characteristic of this novel that Lilly's mother is astonished and yet also "almost dismayed" to see how bravely Lilly

has managed to seem to get over it (ch. 16). Yet if Lilly Dale has sur-
vived her broken heart, she is also fatally damaged by it. Mrs Dale
cannot understand why, obstinately and almost perversely it seems,
Lilly will not turn to Johnny and let herself begin again, as if she
could become a somewhat different person, as we all do through
contingency: Johnny could be to Lilly all that Major Grantly is to
Grace. And he almost does it, never knowing how close he got. For
at one point he really does tempt her to get over her first broken
engagement and lead a second life instead. But on the verge of surrender she suddenly finds herself stubbornly thinking: " – was she in
a moment to be talked out of the resolution of years?" (ch. 78).
"A moment" and "the resolution of years" – it seems so asymmetrical
and yet is also the very way that life works.

Yet on the other hand, as the moment keeps surfacing to offer itself,
it is lovely in Trollope when the older generation, the parents – gradually, reluctantly, resistantly, angrily, but then in an instant, suddenly and
finally – *give in* to the way of things. It is like an extended moment in
the present when life is about to go with the young into the future,
and the parent-figures let themselves begin to go into the past. So,
in *Framley Parsonage*, the grand and formidable Lady Lufton long
resisted her own son's marriage to a lower-class girl until, for love of
her son, "she knew she must yield. She did not say so to herself. She
did not as yet acknowledge that she must put out her hand to Lucy,
calling her by name as her daughter. She did not absolutely say as
much to her own heart; – not as yet" (ch. 43). But the still stubborn
"not as yet" is on the verge of "now," even while not wanting to think
that it is. And when Lady Lufton does go to Lucy, as in surrogate
courtship, to ask her not to refuse her son on her account, then the
old woman has to speak almost from *outside* herself, in order to find a
way to do it: "And as to the stern old mother who thought her only
son too precious to be parted with at the first word – is nothing to be
said to her?" she says to Lucy in wittily dignified surrender, "No for-
giveness to be spoken? ... Is she always to be regarded as stern and
cross, vexatious and disagreeable?" (ch. 46). It is like seeing a small part
of the world changing, remaking and yet still maintaining itself, all at
the same time.

Thus too Archdeacon Grantly, struggling to maintain himself and salvage his dignity, in his unsustainable opposition to the marriage of his son and Grace Crawley:

> it was the nature of the man that when he had been very angry with those he loved, he should be unhappy until he had found some escape from his anger. He could not endure to have to own himself to have been in the wrong, but he could be content with a very incomplete recognition of his having been in the right ... If his son would only drink a glass or two of wine with him comfortably, and talk dutifully about the Plumstead foxes, all should be held to be right, and Grace Crawley should be received with lavish parental embraces ...
>
> "Say something to your father about the property after dinner," said Mrs Grantly to her son when they were alone together.
>
> "About what property?"
>
> "About this property, or any property, you know what I mean; – something to show that you are interested about his affairs. He is doing the best he can to make things right." After dinner, over the claret, Mr Thorne's terrible sin in reference to the trapping of foxes was accordingly again brought up, and the archdeacon became beautifully irate, and expressed his animosity – which he did not in the least feel – against an old friend with an energy which would have delighted his wife, if she could have heard him. (*The Last Chronicle of Barset*, ch. 73)

"Beautifully irate" is itself comically beautiful in its deflection of a big issue into a smaller one, the human "escape" made via a trapped fox. This is a father defeated by his own love, as though ashamed of losing himself in it. For all his principles, he gives in to life but wants to stay in character. And in this passage there is also the wife and mother who long ago, no less than seven hundred pages earlier in chapter 2, had told her husband that he wouldn't have the heart to hold out finally against his son, as he himself well knew. She also told the equally obstinate son, one hundred and fifty pages earlier in chapter 58, that when a man gets what he wants, he should settle without inquiring too "exactly" into the terms of how it has come about. Mrs Oliphant praised the characteristic female position of the woman's "half-amused,

half-troubled spectatorship," her consciousness of the futility of all
decided attempts to set her men-folk right, and her "patient waiting
upon the superior logic of events," as one of those autonomous little
"bits" in the novel "which may scarcely call the attention of the careless reader."[6] And with another little touch as from a different converging level, it is Lady Lufton too who helps the archdeacon to yield,
hearing his complaints but silently thinking "of a certain episode in
her own life" (ch. 56). It is a wonderful tacit mix, once again, of continuity and change. It is almost like a quiet version of Edmund Burke's
grand serial account of what is a nation, whereby in "the great mysterious incorporation of the human race" the whole at any one time
"is never old, or middle-aged or young, but in a condition of unchange-
able constancy," moving on "through the varied tenour of perpetual
decay, fall, renovation, and progression" and thus telling and retelling
the human story.[7]

I love the connection of those "bits" that are left to lie around but
that, when picked up, form a link between different characters in the
same novel, or in the same character across different novels. They are
like bits of time, and they are there anyway within and behind it all,
even when you do not fully register them. They are not dependent on
thought, on conscious recognition. See one or two of those connections
coming to life, and you know there must be a hundred others that will
be there anyway whether you get them or not. What is more, these
connecting "bits" offer a sense of serial cumulativeness in the novel, an
odder phenomenon than one might suppose. You read something about
Mrs Grantly on, say, page 500 and it reminds you of something she said
or did some two hundred pages earlier, you guess, and maybe something
else a hundred pages or so before that – only you made no note of them
at the time because those earlier moments were just below the level of
obvious interest. Yet somehow they have subterraneously built up, created a rich familiarity, by finding on page 500 a future for themselves
dependent upon the reader suddenly half-recalling them from the past.
With Trollope, you as reader live in the plane of the present, created by
the convergence of lives almost meeting up and not quite making it,
even as not quite satisfactorily they carry on forward. And on that
uncompleted plane held together only in time, the reader is free

momentarily to take out one character and trace back the line of his or her story, and then perhaps another; to see relations between two characters that they hardly suspect or cannot clinch; to recognize moments when characters cannot bear to be wholly consistent over time and need something in the present that lies apart from the rest of their lives; thus detecting the constant shift from one interest to another, one fading, another surfacing, all to emerge again later from slightly different angles. It is as if, through the cumulative accretion of implicit familiarity, readers are left alone almost to reassemble the novel themselves as they go along, living with the characters. We take these procedures for granted now, the workings of the classic novel being so intrinsic to our ways of thinking about people. But that readerly reassembling is almost like those bizarre modernist experiments where the writer gave you a set of pages or cards and asked you to put them in any order you liked – except that Trollope leaves the material for experimentation behind for the reader, undemonstrative and unspoken, while he goes sailing on forward in solid and apparently unthinking normality. Line after line he writes out, this time-bound man, 250 words every quarter of an hour between 5.30 and 8.30 each morning, before going on to his work at the post office.

I used to think of Trollope as mechanical, banal, producing a string of stock characters I could look at but never fully identify with. Now I believe that he found a way to create a model that generated life, many lives, regardless of what anyone thought of them, including at times even himself. It didn't matter that it was on the surface a solidly bourgeois world. Beneath that, there were movements that Mrs Oliphant, for example, recognized when she spoke of the "curious consistency and inconsistency" of his people.[8] She was partly thinking of Johnny and Lilly of course but in particular of the great portrait of Crawley himself, unbending in his ruin: for there, as so often with the women in this book, Crawley's wife knows the mixture in her man all too keenly: what is wrong with him comes to her reluctantly, at unpredictable moments, like an unpleasant taste on the palate of her mind, "as such a savour will sometimes, from some unexpected source, come across the palate of the mouth" (ch. 32).

She knew that he was good and yet weak, that he was afflicted by false pride and supported by true pride, that his intellect was still very bright, yet so dismally obscured on many sides as almost to justify people in saying that he was mad. She knew that he was almost a saint, and yet almost a castaway through vanity and hatred of those above him. (*The Last Chronicle of Barset*, ch. 51)

This "almost" man, raging for the want of being just one thing clearly, is greater than those more successful in the church and yet not great enough not to be twisted by his failure. Nor is he assured of either innocence or guilt since he cannot remember how or where he got the stolen check. In the great test, he has to rely blindly on his under-lying character rather than his mind or present consciousness, not knowing if that eroded character withstood its impoverished tempta-tions or in extremity itself blanked out his consciousness of what he was doing. Yet Trollope's paragraph continues without a break beyond those "She knews":

But she did not know that he knew all this of himself also. She did not comprehend that he should be hourly telling himself that people were calling him mad and were so calling him with truth. It did not occur to her that he could see her insight into him.

It is almost too much to bear but in Trollope it is only called "also." For Crawley thinks it too – knows from inside himself all that his wife secretly thinks and fears on his behalf. Yet he still has to be that man, seeing her thinking it. She keeps touching his hand but he wishes he wasn't there. Yet there he is still, physically, in the present. She had urged him to be a man, to bear the trouble bit by bit, and not to keep thinking of his wrongs all the time:

"What else have I that I can think of? Is not all the world against me?"
"Am I against you?"
"Sometimes I think you are. When you accuse me of self-indulgence you are against me." (*The Last Chronicle of Barset*, ch. 12)

To her what she said was meant for his own sake, yet it felt to him as though it were said against him. "Sometimes" is not always: he knows she loves him. But now, at the time, he can only feel it the other way round – that even his greatest friend can speak like one of his enemies. Nothing is quite happening and yet everything is in process – even marriage, the most apparently permanent of relationships, is revealed as made out of different tiny events, almost too momentary to be called events, massed together. Time, so much looser than plot, allows the untidiness, the refuges, and lets in the ill-fitting imperfections. When Mrs Oliphant writes of the mix of "consistency and inconsistency" in Trollope, what those shorthand terms really represent is that interplay in life between the *transient* and the *abiding*, each testing the other out in untidy circumstances that, unresolved, are therefore carried forward. In seeming just to let the process happen without much comment, Trollope the great accepter produces a non-dramatic drama, his readers watching like an audience before a play.

It is to do with getting older of course – the growing to admire Trollope more and more. Much of Victorian literature tells the long, hard story of growing up, given the over-dignified name of Bildungsroman, which, after childhood, nobody can help you with in the way that a parent did or should. Secretly, sometimes humiliatingly, and perhaps even rightly, it goes on much longer than one had ever imagined. As may be seen in this book, I have grown up with Victorian literature, or tried to, seeking shared advice and experience, looking for models or finding parallels, in such as David Copperfield or Maggie Tulliver, not least in the first lonely and naive move from home to university. But the story offered by Trollope instead is the untidy mixture of carrying on and letting go, of something like security and defeat inextricably interconnected, which belongs to the later-middle-aged stage of life. In *The Lay of the Land* (2006) Richard Ford describes it as feeling like the end of "Becoming," when you have become what more or less you now are, however incomplete and still subject to contingency. In Trollope this means taking more of the view from outside, wide-angled, and no longer identifying with a single protagonist or abstracting an ideal of self, consistent and central, from the life around it. It means repetitive truths that are rueful and self-checking, which you think you know, are not surprised by any more, and yet find resurfacing in continuing faults or incorrigible, forgetful self-deceptions as though they were obdurately biological:

> One girl tells another how she has changed her mind in love; and the friend sympathizes with the friend and perhaps applauds. Had the story been told in print, the friend who had listened with equanimity would have read of such vacillation with indignation. She who vacillated herself would have hated her own performance when brought before her judgement as a matter in which she had no personal interest. Very fine things are written every day about honesty and truth, and men read them with a sort of external conviction that a man if he be anything of a man at all, is of course honest and true. But when the internal convictions are brought out between two or three who are personally interested together ... those internal convictions differ very much from the external convictions. (*The Last Chronicle of Barset*, ch. 56)

As the book turns itself almost inside out, this is realist literature warning against literature itself. But it is also the use of another sense, like that sudden blind taste in Mrs Crawley, in order to take thought of the unthinking, of the unsaid and the unadmitted within oneself.

Although they are not the right words to describe Trollope's work, there is something to be said for the sort of stupidity and inarticulacy that lie authentically at the dumb core of a person. Tolstoy's Levin in *Anna Karenina* is that sort of man. It doesn't mean that he isn't also intelligent, but the intelligence comes second.

The Poetic Alternative

Henry Lyte wrote the words to his famous hymn probably around the time in 1847 when he was leaving for the continent to try to recover his health. He died in Nice in the November of that year. The hymn was among those in the first edition of *Hymns Ancient and Modern* (1861) and there, though Lyte himself had written a tune for the words, it was given its best-known accompaniment by the collection's musical editor, William Monk:

> Abide with me; fast falls the eventide;
> The darkness deepens; Lord with me abide!

The lines are long and slow, often in two halves linked by a caesura – a breathing place between the rise and fall of chest and tide alike – rather than any explicit grammatical conjunction such as "because" or "but." The silent gap in the midst is poignant, holding within it the meaning of the whole piece: the fear, the solemn and dying yearning, and the prayer across the great divide. For in these opening lines it goes: permanence in the first half ("abide"), transience in the second half ("fast falls"); followed by a now deepening transience urgently coming first in the line and permanence all the more sought in its second half. I love that turnaround of the order in the different lines, and the developing enjambment from "fast falls the" to "the darkness deepens," just as I love the shift from "Abide with me" at the beginning of the first to "with me abide" at the end of the second, the last word more heart-felt than ever. But the greatest moment, when I hear it, is the almost infinitesimal fraction of a second in the mysterious midst of the line: it's when the call of "Lord" slips slightly *back* across the divide to "The darkness deepens, Lord," in momentary retrospect, before going forward, more consolidated, to "Lord, with me abide."

The poet Douglas Oliver, much missed, used to write about these almost impossible moments in which poetry's time allows habitation: "It is almost as if the emotional and temporally accorded semantic concepts drag the sound directly and sensuously along with them: when we recite well we have almost to *wait* for the right instant to speak each syllable, delaying very minutely durations of vowels to make the tempo perfect."[9] I remember him citing an example from Thomas Hardy's "At Castle Boterel," between the first and second stanzas, and the two of us in a car remembering it together:

> As I drive to the junction of lane and highway,
> And the drizzle bedrenches the waggonette,

I look behind at the fading byway,
    And see on its slope, now glistening wet,
        Distinctly yet

Myself and a girlish form benighted
    In dry March weather.

The past is a sight still just about made out, more like a different world in space-time than just a memory. As Hardy says, a few lines later: "It filled but a minute. But was there ever / A time of such quality, since or before …?" That space – that time – held between "Distinctly yet," at the end of the first stanza, and "Myself and a girlish form," at the opening of the second, is of just such quality. It reaches across the divide between present and past, the sentence pushing forward on the page, but backward in time, in counterpoint with the holding force of rhyme. This, to Douglas Oliver, was time kept alive in poetry as it cannot be in history. The poem is written in March 1913 because that girlish form he courted in March 1870 is now, recently, dead: the bereaved Hardy married her but together they were long unhappy. Now he recalls something other and earlier than the unhappiness that resulted in the ordinary passage of time. Memory is the only alternative Hardy has to Lyte's abiding Lord, unless it is also poetry, which at every reading makes the time just after "Distinctly yet" always stay for a second *and* always pass again. As in a great cadence in music, it feels like a uniquely unrepeatable and almost impossible moment that nonetheless can be repeated, evanescently, at every performance: permanent and transient at once. No wonder Hardy read, though barely comprehended, Einstein on relativity toward the end of his life – Hardy, the last great Victorian hauled into the modern world. He knew how strange it was to live in time.

And always in the background behind Hardy is the older Wessex figure, the dialect poet William Barnes whose beautiful poems on marriage, family, and the mourning of a wife offer the great exemplary narrative of sacramental relationships personally lived out, which Hardy himself must have felt he lacked or even betrayed. Hardy could not go emotionally straight in the way Barnes had. On the road of life, says Barnes, from childhood I looked to being a man, from being a man looked forward to being a husband, then a father: "But now my mind do look behind / Vor jays [For joys]; an' wonder wi' a sigh / When 'twer my jays all pass'd me by" ("Jay A-Pass'd"). But Hardy had even worse turnarounds in his life. What he did understand, as one who had been a novelist as well as poet, was something emotionally and temporally awkward about the formal relation of lines to sentences in poetic counterpoint,[10] especially when reinforced by the shaping powers of rhyme. Here are the opening stanzas of "Your Last Drive," the loss so recent to him that he cannot bear to bury the memory by using "Her" rather than "Your." The shift in which I am interested begins in the sudden dash at line 3, with its retrospective sense of a future, so very close, that the past was unknowingly awaiting:

> Here by the moorway you returned
> And saw the borough lights ahead
> That lit your face – all undiscerned
> To be in a week the face of the dead,
> And you told of the charm of that haloed view
> That never again would beam on you.
>
> And on your left you passed the spot
> Where eight days later you were to lie,
> And be spoken of as one who was not;
> Beholding it with a heedless eye
> As alien from you, though under its tree
> You soon would halt everlastingly.
>
> I drove not with you. ...

What is so powerful here is the movement from the penultimate to the last line of the *first* stanza, and then its equivalent across the first two lines of the *second*. It is like a form of counterpoint between lines and sentences. For the lines here are like time-lines in sentences that are quite consciously almost impossible. Emma Hardy never told her husband about a view that "never again" would beam on her: she simply told him about that view (end-stop), the rest being added by him in painfully ironic afterthought. And of course when she passed (fine word, related to "past") the spot where eight days later she was to lie buried, the whole point is that she could not know that. It is he

96

who now makes the terrible (death-)sentences through second lines that turn those sentences into strange loops. For as so often in Hardy the "last" happens, so to speak, not at the time but only afterward, in realization, when it has gone unmarked. That he did not go with her at the time was characteristic of the separation that so often went on in the latter days of that marriage. But now he wishes he had – though even then, he knows he would not have realized it was the last drive. There should have been a time, a formal reconciliation and farewell, and not just a going, as though in every sense her leaving him.

We are creatures fundamentally unsynchronized with time. In "The Minute Before Meeting," after waiting so long to see a woman whom he knows he will not see again for an equally lengthy period of separation, Hardy finds himself spoiling the moment by having to think "that what is now about to be / Will all *have been* in O, so short a space." Again it is that silent, uninhabitable space in the midst of time that poetry, between the lines, allows Hardy so painfully to inhabit. The words are in monosyllabic slow motion, but speed up as soon as they find their sentence: "about-to-be / Will-all-have-been." The evanescent, in-between space in the fragile present is a mental lacuna, an anomaly beneath our continuing normalities: it is the deep, intractable thing we have to leave behind while we go on, as in Trollope. But the pain of well-nigh unthinkable thoughts piles up in Hardy. This present is also the future of that past; worse, it is often the place where the future, to which the past looked forward, never happened. Retrospect is fallen foreknowledge, coming from the wrong side of time, too late. And there is no real permanence without God. Hardy is a man who would love to be simple – in his downright craftsmanship, in his wish to avoid pain – only to find that would-be simplicity continually caught up again within the unbearably complex and baffling. In the same way, through the added pressure of rhyme the sentences become more complicated than the individual lines that compose them.

There is of course no such lineation in prose, only linear sentences. Yet when it comes to the *reclaiming* of time, one of the most wonderfully representative passages in Victorian literature, too often dismissed as merely sentimental in our low-affect society, is found in Mrs Gaskell's *Cranford* (1853). It is when Miss Matty, last surviving member of the Jenkyns family, goes through old letters with her young friend, Mary Smith. She recalls how, long ago, after a terrible family disagreement with the father, her young brother Peter had run away to sea. Mary Smith narrates:

> We lighted the candle and found the captain's letter and Peter's letter too. And we also found a little simple begging letter from Mrs Jenkyns to Peter, addressed to him at the house of an old schoolfellow, whither she fancied he might have gone. They had returned it unopened; and unopened it had remained ever since, having been inadvertently put by among the other letters of that time. This is it:
>
> > "My dearest Peter,
> > You did not think we should be so sorry as we are, I know, or you would never have gone away. You are too good. Your father sits and sighs till my heart aches to hear him. He cannot hold his head up for grief; and yet he only did what he thought was right. Perhaps he has been too severe, and perhaps I have not been kind enough; but God knows how we love you, my dear only boy. Dor looks so sorry you are gone. Come back and make us happy, who love you so much. I *know* you will come back."
>
> But Peter did not come back. That spring day was the last time he ever saw his mother's face. The writer of the letter – the last – the only person who had ever seen what was written in it, was dead long ago – and I, a stranger, not born at the time when this occurrence took place, was the one to open it. (*Cranford*, ch. 6)

The Victorian is a literature no longer of epic openings or great endings but of middles – even here via a document that at the time was meant to be a means to the end of reconciliation, but is left in suspended animation until Mary Smith opens it up again. That present tense of the letter-writing voice is left as vulnerable as any life in time – lost and unheard, never delivered, accidentally preserved. It did not serve its purpose, it did not serve any purpose after all. "Returned it *unopened; and unopened* it remained" is a syntax that thus marks the suspension of linear movement. And the letter has been "*inadvertently* put by" "*ever* since," as its plea itself was put by in life's unlucky but unerasable accidents. For this is not like the dream-world offered in chapter 45 of Mrs Gaskell's *North and South* (1855) where "every event was measured by the emotions of the mind, not by its actual existence": time is still dominant over what goes on emotionally within it. Thus it is not "your father sits and sighs *till* you come home or *till* I am able to reassure him that you will" but only "sits and sighs *till* my heart aches to hear him. He cannot hold his head up": the time-word "till" offers no dramatic salvation. The writing still goes on *past* the emotion it stirs in a vicarious reader. The reader witnesses Mrs Jenkyns writing in supportive parenthesis: "You did not think we should be so sorry as we are, *I know*, or you would never have gone away"; or delicately inserting with both dignity and concessiveness: "*Perhaps* [your father] has been *too* severe, and *perhaps* I have not been kind *enough*"; a woman neither blaming son nor disparaging husband, but trying to join with both. This is what Mrs Oliphant saw in Trollope – the role of the Victorian woman in the preservation of human feeling.

And yet everyone is dead now. For somewhere further along this line what had seemed a terrible but temporary family row lapsed, then hardened, into a permanent parting without formal *rite de passage*, without anything having happened, its incompleteness now turned into a completed little history only by death. But though it looks like prose fact, the phrase "This is it:" inserted just before the vicarious reading of the letter is really like lineation in poetry, formally signaling the crossing of a threshold into a time that deserves both care and imagination on entry. The writer of the unseen letter was dead, and Mary Smith, a stranger, not even born when all this occurred, was the first to open its memory. It is as though the letter stood for everything that ordinarily goes on between birth and death. And on the other side of the letter is the only response that "I *know* you will come back" ever received: "But Peter did not come back." Another prosaic fact.

This is the story of human life surrendered to earthly time, for want of synchronization. The mother never got to her son:

> "And she was too late," said Miss Matty; "too late!" We sat in silence, pondering on the full meaning of those sad, sad words. At length I asked Miss Matty to tell me how her mother bore it. (*Cranford*, ch. 6)

That hush acts like the actual silence created by lineation in poetry, to do service to the meaning of "too late, too late," matched by the left-over feeling of "sad, sad." It is an image of the temporal *half*-rescue-work of the ordinary that Victorian literature so often exists to provide. And it is deliberately and scrupulously only half a rescue, not changing the actual outcome, but at least ensuring that the feeling of loss is itself not lost. Though at the time the emotions did no good either to those who felt them or to those for whose sake they were felt, it is undeserved that the value of those cares, unvalidated by successful outcomes, should go unrecognized. I am fed up with hearing vicarious literary feeling dismissed as writer's manipulativeness or reader's parasitism. Vicarious literary emotion is more like the overspill of what will not go *into* time *at* the time, of all that has insufficient room for itself in the physical constrictions of the world. That lost dimension is literature's own. The ideal would be the magic of *A Christmas Carol* (1843) in its redemption of time and its recall of emotion. For by the end of the tale Scrooge can live in the present, past and future together, waking to find that it is still Christmas Day and no time has been wasted. And for once, the protagonist himself is turned into his own vicarious spectator; old Scrooge is made into the reader of his own life. That means that those external emotions he experiences when he has to witness his past, present, and future selves are turned back *inside* himself to remake and redeem his story. It is the story of how vicarious emotion might not be wasted, might not be too late, after all. That is important when most literary emotion – I mean, the emotion stirred in us by literature – is vicarious. I do not want to think that literary emotion has no relation to reality save as artificial and belated compensation for all that is unfelt in life itself. Literature is a holding-ground in which to think about life – for those who have no other place to go to, in order to do so. And within that holding-ground, like the arena created for Scrooge by a spirit, or like the taut rhymed space that Hardy creates, there are reminders.

★

Yet, startlingly, this kind of supportive humanism is *not* what Victorian poetry mainly aspires to. For the first time in English literary history, the novel was becoming the dominant cultural mode, in poetry's place. The Victorian poets were thus the first group of writers to begin to feel that what they were doing was perhaps unnecessary, redundant, and out of touch with modern life in a way that the realist social novel was not. I want to say that there was in that development an equivocal freedom for the poets, a sense of strangeness that was disturbed and disturbing.

For example: when you read the bare, seemingly transcripted words of a dramatic monologue by Robert Browning, it is like reading an experimental novel with the narrator and the scenery all taken away. You have to infer where the speaker is coming from; with uncertainty you have to fill in both the surrounding and the background context, even as you must continue overhearing the foreground shifts and changes. It is like meeting a stranger and having to try to understand him without signposts in orientation; like hearing without quite seeing in context; like trying to guess the whole from the present little part. It aspires to be more realist than the realist novel.

And the Victorian sequence poem – the great Victorian discovery, or rediscovery after the models of Dante's *Vita Nuova* or Petrarch's sonnets to Laura – is a variation on that alternative to the novel. For the sequence poem tells a story in a series of lyrics, *and* in the spaces in between them, without a novel's surrounds. It lives tonally moment by present moment, while interrogating itself as to where it has got to, or what it is, or how it now relates to its own past and future, even as it goes along. The great examples are Elizabeth Barrett Browning's *Sonnets from the Portuguese* (privately printed 1847, published 1850), Arthur Hugh Clough's "Amours de Voyage" (1858), George Meredith's *Modern Love* (1862), Christina Rossetti's "Monna Innominata" and "Later Life" (both 1881), Dante Gabriel Rossetti's "The House of Life" (1870, further expanded 1881), Tennyson's *In Memoriam* (composed from 1833, published 1850), and latterly Thomas Hardy's "Poems of 1912–13." The shiftingness of some of these dates of composition itself indicates the intrinsic provisionality, the revisionary nature of the enterprise.

For these poems take the great traditional "types," the classifactory human norms or templates, and against those apparently permanent, static ideals inherited from the past, keep asking themselves from inside any given present: "Is *this* what is called Love?" "Is *this* what Marriage is meant to be like?" "Is *this* how Death is supposed to be borne?" It is what Walter Bagehot called "the type in difficulties," the immutable idea giving way to the testing processes of changing experience in the nineteenth century.[11] These are temporal and hence secular difficulties, about love lasting within the form of permanent marriage, about life going on perhaps pointlessly after so much has gone dead within it. What world is this now? Poetry may not have felt as rooted in the common world as did the realist novel. But its very sensitiveness to the predicament of estrangement, of insecure disloca- tion, of the vulnerability of existence becomes an expression of the age's own hidden difficulties with itself. Such poetry is the alternative to Trollope's solidity, in its apprehension of a fleeting yet recurring sense of present disorientation or unplaceableness, without a secure human framework.

"I wish I could remember that first day," writes Christina Rossetti to her beloved, "First hour, first moment of your meeting me" ("Monna Innominata," 2). "So unrecorded did it slip away" – because it wasn't a beginning, as it were, until it turned out to have been so later. "It seemed to mean so little, meant so much."

"Not solely that the Future she destroys," writes George Meredith from the other end of the story, contemplating what his wife's adul- tery means to their grotesquely continuing marriage (*Modern Love*, 12). It is not just the future that is at stake as though time could ever be straightforwardly linear for human beings:

> Methinks with all this loss I were content,
>> If the mad Past, on which my foot is based
> Were firm, or might be blotted ...

The past on which everything has been based is now also shaken by and in this present. That is why it feels "mad," with the present dissolving what the protagonist only now realizes he had so assumed to be the firm story of his life. "Where began the change ...?" (*Modern Love*, 10).

These people do not know where they are, do not know if this baf- fled present is part of anything more, or is anything at all even in itself. It is not even a transition, unless it later becomes seen as such rather than a dead end. And this is where the Victorian period is so powerful – again, in that in-between area that is unable to ease itself by simply

102

giving up on ideas of solidity or structures of story and yet experiences the present as all the more strange for want of those groundings and categories. Elizabeth Barrett was a 40-year-old spinster still living in the family home, who thought herself plain, had suffered grave illness, and felt herself half-dead after the death of her brother. "Guess now who holds thee?" says a voice. "Death," she replies. Life answers back, "Not Death, but Love" (*Sonnets from the Portuguese*, 1). Yet she can hardly believe these names – the sudden experience is more like Christina Rossetti's use of "somewhat" or "something" in "Later Life" (1880):

> We lack, yet cannot fix upon the lack:
> Not this, nor that; yet somewhat, certainly.
> (sonnet 6)

> Something this foggy day, a something which
> Is neither of this fog nor of to-day.
> (sonnet 17)

This is poetry written in the dark. Elizabeth Barrett's own most definable emotion in the midst of unreliable change is something close to fear, itself braver and more authentic than simple gratitude or fixed delight would have been. She is losing her old life, however bad it has been, for a life that she can hardly trust, that may not last, and that even so she may never be able to get over: the very line-endings in her verse are like the stuttering of liminal experience:

> Nevermore
> Alone upon the threshold of my door
> Of individual life, I shall command
> The uses of my soul
> (*Sonnets from the Portuguese*, 6)

She will no longer ever be single, even within herself, whether he stays with her or passes away like a dream. But if it isn't an abortive beginning, it is the new life and self that Lilly Dale resisted, that Lucy Snowe in Charlotte Bronte's *Villette* disguised her own despairing desire for. Yet because it takes Elizabeth Barrett out of both the family and the familiar, the emotions are strange to her and unpredictable and rawly new – not just feelings like joy, but more the feeling of feelings, like fear of joy:

> If I leave all for *thee*, wilt thou exchange
> And *be* all to me? Shall I never miss
> Home-talk and blessing and the common kiss
> That comes to each in turn, nor count it strange
> When I look up, to drop on a new range
> Of walls and floors, ... another home than this?
> (*Sonnets from the Portuguese*, 35)

Her lover was of course the poet Robert Browning. "My life was ended when I knew you," she writes to him January 17, 1846, herself suddenly made young in age. "I had done *living*, I thought, when you came & sought me out" (September 18, 1845). But life for her is not that shape, has not that structure it seems: as it now goes on in the experimental mix of things, if it is not at an end after all, it must perhaps be a beginning. Yet she finds herself still having to think from inside her newly old self (April 9, 1846): "How dreadfully natural it would be if you did leave off loving me." "You see in me what is not," she tells him (September 16, 1845), fearful of psychological projection, "and overlook in me what is unsuitable to you." "But I believe in *you* absolutely, utterly," he had said from the first, offering what is crucially a language of faith: "My first & last word – I *believe* in you."[12]

My colleague Josie Billington, once one of the original members of the part-time Victorian MA, asks a question prompted by reading the real-life correspondence between Elizabeth and Robert Browning: why did Elizabeth Barrett feel the need to say in the unconsummated dialogue of poetry what she was already saying in recognizably similar language in the letters? Josie Billington's answer is this: "New life and new self felt nervously unprotected by the love which had created them." She goes on: "If this potential self had not self-belief enough as yet to support its own emergence, the poetry offered a form in which this coming-to-life self could reside ahead of its full and secure realisation in her."[13] The poetry is what the poet herself calls "a place to stand and love in" – where she can say "*I love thee ... mark! ... I love thee,*" realizing it to herself as well as to him in the very act of the renewed repetition (*Sonnets from the Portuguese*, 10). In poem 33 she had told her lover to call her by her pet-name from childhood and across all the years she will come running "with the same heart," mending any breaks or transitions. Yet it is exactly that phrase that is picked up at the beginning of poem 34 – "With the same heart, I said" – only to give way to the question: "Is the same, the same?" She is no longer a child; some of those who called her by the old name are now dead; it is now a different kind of intimacy from family love. And yet there may also be some kind of renewed continuity. This is how the poems, listening to themselves and picking up their own words a moment later in their own time, strugglingly hold themselves together in the equivocal mix of sameness and difference.

Dante Gabriel Rossetti puts it brilliantly in offering a language for the way in which the sequence may gradually develop a complex life and ancestry of its own:

> As growth of form or momentary glance
>   In a child's features will recall to mind
>   The father's with the mother's face combin'd,
> Sweet interchange that memories still enhance:
> And yet, as childhood's years and youth's advance,
>   The gradual mouldings leave one stamp behind
>   Till in the blended likeness now we find
> A separate man or woman's countenance:–
> So in the Song, the singer's Joy and Pain,
>   Its very parents, ever more expand.
>   ("Transfigured Life," *The House of Life*, 60)

Joy and Pain in the make-up of the poem become like the face of father and of mother: gradually in time they merge and blend to make a new face out of the combination of its parents, forming features and memories of its own. These poems no longer have simple names – joy or pain. For they are about strange and complex compounds of unsettling and barely definable experiences unassimilated as yet within the classic patterns of emotion. There is Elizabeth Barrett Browning's fear

105

of hope; there is Meredith's inner disgust at his own bitterness, Tennyson's love lost in the apparent *non*-feelings of depressive grief. As an alternative to the desired, elusive, or half-lost type-feeling used to clarify and inhabit the poem's own situation, these feelings *about* feelings are part of the Victorians' interest in new, second-order patterns. For this is the first age interested in genetics, in the complex amalgams and evolved hybrids that make up new created things, changing the old rules.

In this uncharted experience, there is no supportive narrator in this present and no reassuring grounding in a narrative past tense. In a sequence poem's stops and starts, there is no knowing what is passing mood, what is permanent feeling, and no criteria for calling or not calling an emotion genuine:

> What words are these have fall'n from me?
>   Can calm despair and wild unrest
>   Be tenants of a single breast
> Or sorrow such a changeling be?
> (In Memoriam, 16)

This is Tennyson on mourning. You can feel its symptoms: the immediate self-questionings in struggle with an available language that may hide as much as it tells even in the moment of utterance ("sorrow"?); the hopelessly changing feelings themselves now disturbingly distinct from the missing person to whom they still refer. There is the incongruousness of the mood-shift ("calm despair and wild unrest"); the inability to measure what if anything is deepest or most true: in short, the paradoxically much-felt *un*reality of it all.

Like a culmination of the problems of Victorian poetry, *In Memoriam* has no beginning, no clear overall form save that of a poetic diary, no event as such that can bring it to an end. For it exists *after* an ending, after the sudden, unexpected early death of Tennyson's friend Arthur Hallam, so that its subject-matter is not there, but missing and missed. Hallam died young, suddenly, of a brain hemorrhage abroad: Tennyson was not even there physically to see it, only to hear about it afterward in disbelief. Death shocks time: the young life is at once finite and yet also incomplete. "Loss is common," someone tells Tennyson in poem 6, but paradoxically what is common here does not exist at the level of commonality; it exists as individual, in separation from the outer world, muffled within the dull metric beat of inner loss. Instead of direct solidities, there is instead the strange time-lag of the left-over feeling involved in mourning, no longer in time with the normal world or in touch with it, beset by second-order feelings cut off from the lost external world in strange, depressed combinations of living death. Yet in the midst of such disorientation, what this poem can do is find a syntax by which to *have* a thought ahead of knowing what to *do* with it, or where it will take you, or to what framework it belongs:

> The wish, that of the living whole
> No life may fail beyond the grave

There it is, "*The* wish," however vulnerable, put up front like incorrigible human matter, before being worked into sense through the poem's characteristic questions and negatives, themselves turned to would-be positive effect wherever possible:

> Derives it not from what we have
> The likest God within the soul?
> (*In Memoriam*, 55)

Under that pressure, "that is most like" becomes "The likest" (close too, in its compression, to no more than "the likeliest"): "The ... the ... the" is poetry struggling to get a hold on things, its verbal inventions produced more by a sense of struggling amorphousness than by creative freedom.

And the movement from stanza to stanza is like crossing by stepping-stones, with unknown gaps in between. For in the poem's provisionality, the little word "then" in the next stanza of poem 55 is what the poet holds onto, to ask himself the question that follows: how does this thought (that the strong human wish for an afterlife may be a trace of God within us) fit in relation to the other great Victorian name-word, Nature, the other competing framework of Victorian understanding in the hands of the evolutionists? No soul shall perish finally, says Religion. The individuals shall all go and must all go, says Nature, it is only species themselves that need to be kept going.

> Are God and Nature then at strife,
>> That Nature lends such evil dreams?
>> So careful of the type she seems,
> So careless of the single life;
>
> That ...
>
> (*In Memoriam*, 55)

Tennyson is going to say, almost stutteringly, in another four lines' time "I falter where I firmly trod.""So careful ... So careless" becomes "That I ...": the sequence forces the man on along his honest journey even to that realization of its uncertainty; a recognition arrived at always *just* belatedly across lines and stanzas. Tennyson is like a slow thinker because every thought feels as though it is a blow or an unsurety.

Thus after seven more lines of 55, lyric 56 begins with the poet looking back on the immediate past of his own poem in writing-time, re-quoting what he has just said of Nature in her ruthless evolutionary process – and then forcing himself to go one step further again:

> "So careful of the type?" but no.
>> From scarped cliff and quarried stone
>> She cries, "A thousand types are gone:
> I care for nothing, all shall go."

It is another of the poem's strange loops that even the meaninglessness of blind Nature's non-humanity is still only expressible for us within human language, ironically itself perhaps no more than a chance evolutionary product. That is why the only thing the poet can do at these limits of sense is put down his words in rough provisionality, and see where they lead, or leave them till later. Maybe the thought that arises cannot be used: it may have gone beyond where you can immediately follow, or fallen short of where you want to be, seeming a dead end. That is how Tennyson precariously makes his long poem out of this series of little ones. Why can't we believe we are going to die? If it is God the answer is: because we aren't – and the wish is validated? But if it is Nature: because we are – and we don't want to accept it?

And what about Man? Again a subject is presented at the beginning of a lyric without a syntax yet that knows what to do it. Man like Nature's last work goes on persistently; Man who trusted God, and believed the universe existed finally for benign purposes compatible with humanity. Then comes Tennyson's question: – shall he

> Who loved, who suffer'd countless ills
>   Who battled for the True, the Just,
>   Be blown about the desert dust,
> Or seal'd within the iron hills?
> (*In Memoriam*, 56)

But that "shall he" was spoken two stanzas earlier and then held back, anticipating the future of the thought. When the main verb does finally come, it serves only to make the transition from "the True, the Just" to "Be blown about the desert dust" all the more terribly close: abruptly near-ungrammatical across the gap between one line and the next, it is all the more terrifyingly meaningless.

Tennyson would periodically re-read and review his poem in the course of its composition. Whenever he found what seemed like a blank space in the sequence, he inserted a poem. Writing one lyric required him to write another that seemed missing, that seemed to occupy some space implicit between previous poetic diary entries. He would work away between already written lyrics, opening up spaces of possibility he had made but left, or working within disturbing holes to find inference and anomaly. In many ways the writing was accidental, moody, interrupted, discontinuous, adventitious. And yet if something in the way of discovery or recovery came out of that, if the poems seemed somehow called for in the spaces they made and filled, and thus began to find a way or make a whole, then chance itself would be transformed and would become something closer to hidden destiny.

Others may be right to prefer the intense linguistic inventiveness of Gerard Manley Hopkins's terrible sonnets, written around 1883, with all their absolute extremity. "No worst, there is none. Pitched past pitch of grief / More pangs will, schooled at forepangs, wilder wring." But for me it is the normality of mind that Tennyson retains within the abnormal, a limited man continuing for years in a situation beyond him, which is the achievement of the sequence – *as* sequence that the man has to live with and live through.

Indeed, the most chastening achievement of *In Memoriam* is that all the strangeness and experimentalism exist *not* to discover something newer, better, or other than the old Judeo-Christian faith to which the poet was so scared of predictably resorting only for comfort's sake. The poem is rather a means by which that faith rediscovers itself as stranger, inside, than a conventional language had ever allowed it to be. Tennyson starts poem 125:

> That which we dare invoke to bless;
>   Our dearest faith; our ghastliest doubt;
>   He, They, One, All; within, without;
> The Power in Darkness whom we guess

Again the great unspeakable subject is bravely up front, even as "guess." But then the next stanza must ask: where can you find this many-named nameless presence? Not in the beauty of the world, not in the logical argument of design, is the reply; instead, in that area where doubt and faith are not as separate as they sound. An inner voice threatens "Believe no more" and Tennyson wants to stand up to it like a man – but "No, like a child in doubt and fear" is what he is. It feels like a defeat – but then:

> Then was I as a child that cries,
> But, crying, knows his father near;
>
> And what I am beheld again
>   What is, and no man understands;
>   And out of darkness came the hands
> That reach thro' nature, moulding men.

110

It is the crying that is the breakthrough, not the manliness. I don't think that's regression: I think it is a recognition that the claims for adulthood are often a frail defense and pretense, in willed assertion of an autonomy that must try to remain unemotional. The cry of this child helps find, but not bring, the father. But then at the next step, beyond the human, it gives way to the language of "what": "What I am" in relation to "What is" and "That which." When the old words – God, Religion, the Soul, Love, the True, and the Just – sound like empty human inventions, then whatever they stood for, if there at all, had to be found again in the dark by a poetry saying "What is, *and* no man understands."

To imagine by means of such Braille-like language is like trying to look through the "glimmering square" Tennyson describes in "Tears idle tears," a song from *The Princess* (1847) that for a moment imagines the sadness and the strangeness of a death-bed:

> as in dark summer dawns
> The earliest pipe of half-awaken'd birds
> To dying ears, when unto dying eyes
> The casement slowly grows a glimmering square

Still honestly held between vision and hallucination, between closing down and opening up, this is the Victorian mortal at the very edge of time, trying to see what if anything lies beyond it. T. S. Eliot knew that Tennyson relied upon his doubt as much as his faith, and that of the two it was his doubt that was almost the more religious: so it was to be too in Eliot's own religious sequence poem, *Four Quartets*.

5

Individual Agents

Admired by the influential Goethe, translated by George Eliot and Mark Rutherford, the Dutch seventeenth-century philosopher Spinoza is a powerful presence in the intellectual history of Victorian England. In his *Ethics*, for example, he described emotion as "a confused idea," "an inadequate idea" – that is to say, a thought imprisoned in feeling such that we experience its effect on us, in a blur of intense responsiveness, without truly understanding its cause.[1] Emotions happen to us; their passion (as the word's etymology suggests) is something we suffer. And whatever we suffer somewhat diminishes us, in taking from us the power of action. Melancholy sadness, in particular, marks the passage to a lesser state, our strength of feeling turned against us in depression like a sort of innerly sapping poison. But if we can find the cause of this effect, can set free the thought trapped or distorted within the personal feeling, then we are closer to acting than suffering. We are transformed from simply being ourselves to being able to think *about* ourselves. Those thoughts might still not be as adequate, objective, or fully rational as Spinoza had hoped. But as one of Saul Bellow's troubled intellectual protagonists, Herzog, puts it in direct address to the philosopher: "Thoughts not causally connected were said by you to cause pain. I find that is indeed the case."[2] Herzog wants those thoughts to be objects, verbally, in front of his eyes for him to work upon, making them a subject-matter and not just an unseen inner burden. He wants to *make* something of his experience, and not just to have it.

For another admirer of Spinoza, Matthew Arnold, the ability to think out in writing – in particular the active articulation involved in the creation of poetry – was always the crucial sign of the capacity to transcend personal helplessness, and move from passive to active. What in Arnold's eyes distinguished Chaucer, for example, from contemporary French romance poets was Chaucer's command of a view of the whole of life: "Chaucer had not their helplessness," he writes in "The Study of Poetry," "he has gained the power to survey the world from a central, from a truly human point of view." In his preface to the first edition of his *Poems* (1853), Arnold spoke of the effort equivalently to attain "the mastery of the great artists." In the preface to his play *Merope* (1858), he said that the poetry to be found even amidst the suffering of Greek tragedy "offered a lofty sense of the mastery of the human spirit over its own stormiest agitations." "Mastery" was a word for that desire of his to get out from under:

> Plainness and clearness without shadow of stain!
> Clearness divine!
> Ye heavens, whose pure dark regions have no sign
> Of languor, though so calm, and, though so great,
> Are yet untroubled and unpassionate;
> Who, though so noble, share in the world's toil,
> And, though so task'd, keep free from dust and soil!
> I will not say that your mild deeps retain
> A tinge, it may be, of their silent pain
> Who have long'd deeply once, and long'd in vain –
> But I will rather say that you remain
> A world above man's head, to let him see
> How boundless might his soul's horizons be,
> How vast, yet of what clear transparency!
> How it were good to abide there, and breathe free ...
> ("A Summer Night")

Arnold saw a world harassed by a thousand practicalities, where bustle was a parody of action. He saw a stifled people (as he wrote to his friend Arthur Hugh Clough, December 1847) "prevailed over by the world's multitudinousness," scattered into restless fragmentation where (as Arnold put it in "The Scholar-Gipsy") "each half lives a hundred different lives." The poet who also diligently traveled the country as a school inspector,

113

compiling his reports toward a more educated nation of the future, still did not see how to "share in the world's toil" and yet "keep free from dust and soil." What he wanted was a quietist sky-place, a primary forgotten but beautiful world "above men's heads," which was pure, calm, clear, wide, not inhuman in its tinges of remembered pain, yet untroubled by lower passion. It was a world, like poetry, to breathe free in.

Arnold hated the merely practical requirements of a narrow-minded materialist work-ethic, with all the repeatedly ugly philistine demands as to the *use* of doing anything other than what was immediately profitable. And poetry was all the more important for Arnold because in his eyes the realist novel, which was threatening to replace it, could never be sufficient: it was art in surrender to the outside world. But if, as Arnold put it to himself in his preface, nothing in his own poetry was actually *done*, if the suffering expressed "found no vent in action," then for all his high ideals for poetry (and perhaps because of them), he was merely playing into the hands of culture's opponents. "Spinoza," Arnold wrote in a piece on the thinker in *Essays in Criticism*, first series, "has made his distinction between adequate and inadequate ideas a current notion for educated Europe." To see the need for something other than materialism, to try to fill that need, and then, after all that, not to be able to do so was the Arnoldian dilemma, so characteristic of his time. That is why he honored the Stoic Roman emperor Marcus Aurelius, who, through the writing of his *Meditations*, was able to live on *less* than his capacities required or suggested, on less than enough.

If Arnold's was no more than the weakened poetry of defeated idealist yearning, then it was as though – in the words of another of Saul Bellow's men in the tough materialism of twentieth-century Chicago – "to be a poet is a school thing, a skirt thing, a church thing."[3] An old-hat thing too, if, in its embarrassed spirituality, poetry is just a second-order aesthetic hangover from religion. Bellow's narrator hears in the next century the ebbing of the Sea of Faith that Arnold himself recorded in "Dover Beach" – the "melancholy, long withdrawing roar / Retreating":

> The ideas of the last few centuries are used up. . . . The greatest things, the things most necessary for life, have recoiled and retreated. People are

actually dying of this, losing all personal life, and the inner being of millions, many many millions, is missing. (*Humboldt's Gift*, p. 244)

Bellow is here thinking of the failed poet Delmore Schwartz, who lost his poetry and himself.[4] The late Ian Hamilton, himself a poet who wrote less than he knew he should have, said that the deepest impulse in Arnold's own poetry was a repudiation "of those very elements in his own nature which urged him towards poetry in the first place."[5] What *is* all this about literature and art and culture saving lives? It is not good if idealism sounds like nineteenth-century ivory-towered rhetoric, if humanist piety becomes the unreal public language of those who privately fail. Instead of the hollowness of insistent prophetic stress, Arnold's own prose employs deft strategies of irony and satire. But the problem inherited by Saul Bellow's men cannot be long evaded: namely, the heavy claims made for literature as though it could be a replacement, in the inner life, for religion.

In his novel about Dickens, *The Mutual Friend*, published in 1978, Frederick Busch tells a story about Matthew Arnold that I think he must have made up, since I can find it nowhere, but that speaks a truth about how Arnold tried to maintain himself. One day, Busch tells us, Arnold was in his study, trying to write a poem. Outside there was a team of workmen noisily carrying out repairs. The quietist poet could not bear it. Eventually he went out to speak to the men. But before he could so, remarkably, one of the workmen recognized him. "Are you Matthew Arnold?" he asked. To which the reply was: "Not yet." Not yet, because if the poem was left off in semi-draft, Arnold was not what he called "himself," his real or best self:

> But often, in the world's most crowded streets,
> But often, in the din of strife,
> There rises an unspeakable desire
> After the knowledge of our buried life;
> A thirst to spend our fire and restless force
> In tracking out our true, original course;
> A longing to inquire
> Into the mystery of this heart which beats
> So wild, so deep in us – to know

115

Whence our lives come and where they go.
And many a man in his own breast then delves,
But deep enough, alas! none ever mines.
And we have been on many thousand lines
And we have shown, on each, spirit and power;
But hardly have we, for one little hour,
Been on our own line, have we been ourselves –
("The Buried Life")

"But often, but often; but deep enough, alas; hardly; for one *little* hour."
For once here, Arnold *does* make the concerns of poetry into the
problems of a wider need for human self-expression. In the very
middle of the busy modern world, depressed frustration is a sign that
there is something buried in us that is vitally questioning of fundamental origins and primary purposes; that needs to stay down in the
depths weighted by a language of sufficient seriousness but released
by its words. *What can I do?* (the great question in *Middlemarch*
"capable by varied vocal inflexions of expressing all states of mind
from helpless dimness to exhaustive argumentative perception")[6] is
the characteristic cry of all that the Victorian age stands for. What can
I *do*, what can I *be*, what can I *say?* "For most men in a brazen prison
live" ("A Summer Night"). The existential need and the stifled potential are what poetic expressiveness represents in those who can never
be poets as such, but still must find "their own line" somewhere.

Amidst all the difficulties of public discourse and spiritual mission,
this chapter is about personal vocation, the need to find one's own line,
with that wonderful homing poetic stress laid upon "own." It is about
the Victorian individual seeking some freedom from the common prison of passivity; it is about the Victorian belief in the individual voice.

★

But this time the individuals in which I am interested are neither
poets nor novelists but the non-fiction writers of the age, belong-
ing by choice, failure, duty, or frustration to an unnamed, pre-
professionalized, unspecialized category somewhere in between artists
and philosophers.

Goethe the poet felt that the austere philosopher Spinoza was, as it were, the *other side* of himself – coming, by means of external abstract reason, at what Goethe reached through a language of inner experience, as from a parallel universe. George Eliot's partner George Henry Lewes quoted Goethe on the electric charge of meaning he felt between the two of them: "The all-equalising calmness of Spinoza was in striking contrast with my all-disturbing activity; his mathematical method was the direct opposite of my poetic style of thought ... Mind and heart, understanding and sense, sought each other with eager affinity, binding together the most different natures."[7] Goethe had no doubt that each could and should be translated into the other, in the name of the wholeness of life. Emotion must find within itself the explicit thought it experientially contained. But what it *felt* like to *have* a thought, humanly embodied, was the thought's final meaning in the world. To be both poet and philosopher, to have thoughts about feelings, and feelings about thoughts, was George Eliot's double ambition.

But I am interested here in those who through their individuality create and by their presence hold onto the place *in between* supposedly distinct mental faculties or separate cultural disciplines, in the rich, non-specialist, common-language world of the nineteenth century. Arnold, Mill, Carlyle, Ruskin, Newman use artistic gifts translated into areas and discourses outside art. In their different ways and beliefs, they embed what may seem like abstract reasoning or ideological argument in what is actually experience and autobiography, the story of a person trying to think in relation to the perceived world.

John Stuart Mill's *On Liberty* (1859) exists precisely to defend such individualism. For like so many distinctive Victorian voices, Mill's is in one sense also anti-Victorian. He looks at a world where people are frightened into mass conformity:

> Not only in what concerns others, but in what concerns only themselves, the individual or the family do not ask themselves – what do I prefer? or, what would suit my character and disposition? or, what would allow the best and highest in me to have fair play, and enable it to grow and thrive? They ask themselves, what is suitable to my position?

117

what is usually done by persons of my station and pecuniary circumstances? or (worse still) what is usually done by persons of a station and circumstances superior to mine? I do not mean that they choose what is customary, in preference to what suits their own inclination. It does not occur to them to have any inclination, except for what is customary. (*On Liberty*, III, "Of Individuality, as One of the Elements of Well-being")

By dint of not following their nature, they end up having no nature to follow and becoming second-order people as a result. One might think such people were living in a world of political oppression and tyrannical censorship. But the ostensibly free modern world of democracy and materialism, says Mill, exerts its pressures by more subtly deceptive, *indirect* means – by social forces, to do with imitative fashion, comforting conformity, and the safety of acceptable mediocrity; forces that go all the deeper for being more subtly unconscious and less clearly visible than physical or legal constraints. At least in the ancient world men and women knew if they were slaves, could see and feel if they were deprived of rights or forced into obedience. But now conformity happens both without their knowing and as though by their consent. Formerly, moreover, "different ranks, different neighbourhoods, different trades and professions, lived in what might be called different worlds; at present, to a great degree in the same" (ibid.). Now, through the power of the Industrial Revolution, the key tendency in Mill's eyes is "assimilation": through democratic political changes, national education, improved and more rapid communication systems, increased opportunities for acquiring money and status, the world is become smaller, less varied, and more uniformly geared to its material molds and purposes. For all its industry, it is to Mill increasingly a deadened world of false and tame certainties. It doesn't want to hear negative logic point out weaknesses in theory or errors in practice, unless the skepticism can at once be absorbed into the reestablishment of positive truths. It is fearful of forms of energy that do not immediately fit in with the frameworks of established convention. For the sake of social cohesion, it is therefore institutionally suppressive of life and individuality – which increasingly have to become synonymous. "Originality is the one thing which unoriginal minds cannot feel the use of" (*On Liberty*, III).

When ethical or religious creeds are *first* fighting for their existence, said Mill, "they are full of meaning and vitality to those who originate them, and to the direct disciples of their originators" (*On Liberty*, II):

> But when it has come to be an hereditary creed, and to be received passively not actively – when the mind is no longer compelled, in the same degree as at first, to exercise its vital powers on the questions which its belief presents to it, there is a progressive tendency to forget all of the belief except the formularies, or to give it a dull and torpid assent, as if accepting it on trust dispensed with the necessity of realizing it in consciousness, or testing it by personal experience; until it almost ceases to connect itself at all with the inner life of the human being. (*On Liberty*, II)

This is how the majority of mid-nineteenth-century believers held the doctrine of Christianity, Mill argued, as it were *outside* the mind, "encrusting and petrifying it against all other influences addressed to the higher parts of our nature." That secondariness is, again, the price paid for civilization and for those general benefits involved in the inherited acceptance of virtues that had once to fight for their place in the world. But to *realize* a belief as if for the first time again, to hold it *inside* the mind and keep it living and renewed, to make it something received not passively but *actively*: all this requires one who is genuinely an individual – indeed, has need of "a succession of persons whose ever-recurring originality prevents the grounds of those beliefs and practices from becoming merely traditional" (*On Liberty*, III). The teachers of mankind, Mill concluded, are those who make education a counter to unthinking tradition, by submitting it to the challenges of a continuous, questioning dialogue: "He who knows only his own side of the case, knows little of that." Out of a hundred so-called educated people ninety-nine are in this condition: "Their conclusion may be true, but it might be false for anything they know: they have never thrown themselves into the mental position of those who think differently from them." In their desire for false but easy security they dare not think with Mill that "the beliefs which we have most warrant for, have no safeguard to rest on, but a standing invitation to the whole world to prove them unfounded" (*On Liberty*, II). The tenets of Mill's radical liberal creed are thus:

> That mankind are not infallible; that their truths, for the most part, are only half-truths; that unity of opinion, unless resulting from the fullest and freest comparison of opposite opinions, is not desirable, and diversity not an evil, but a good, until mankind are much more capable than at present of recognizing all sides of the truth. (*On Liberty*, III)

"Of Individuality" in particular meant a lot to Thomas Hardy, for example: in its encouragement of diverse "experiments of living," Mill's chapter offered him the sense of a space in which to be off-centre, against the swim, even in his apparent nay-saying.

The tolerance for a variety of individual points of view, each absolute to the individual in question, characterized the overall relativism of *On Liberty*. That split-level agnostic mix of the relative and the absolute, showing also as the social and the personal, was characteristic of the period at both its richest and its most confused. It seemed to many of Mill's opponents, however, that Mill had a secret, secular agenda, in undercover opposition to the Christian society of Victorian England. Experiments in living were to such critics no more than adventures in a two-fold incoherence. First: from where were these supposedly distinct individuals to get these new ideas of theirs? Second: what would hold together a genuine society if it consisted merely of a loose mix of private, pluralist views? To others amongst Mill's critics the commitment to allowing and encouraging diversity was, in the words of the *British Quarterly Review*, at best a "negative creed," a second-order tolerance.[8] What Mill was offering seemed not so much a belief *per se* as a belief that there should be many beliefs. This meant for R. H. Hutton – the best *reader* amongst Victorian literary critics – that ironically Mill was not himself an individual, but a mind, apparently rational and impartial. Newman spoke of writers' individual styles accompanying their thoughts and beliefs as inevitably and involuntarily as their own shadow, but Mill, said Hutton, had no personal style at all, his strategy being to present himself as the "impersonal intelligence" of the age in its developing historical progress toward a more emancipated future.[9] That lofty perspective, said Hutton, was "for those who were able to look down, not for those who felt themselves looked down upon."[10] In their different ways both Arnold in poetry and Mill in philosophy are testimony to that increasingly secularized need for an overview of the world created even from within it. But for Hutton the more honorably true position of the age lies in the plight of those who feel themselves creatures struggling between heaven and earth. They still felt themselves looked down upon – even from some point they could briefly imagine though not steadily attain; even if at times it felt that there was No One there any more to do the seeing. For Hutton it was that creaturely feeling, closer to insecurity than to autonomy, which marked what it soberly felt like to be no more and no less than an individual in the world.

★

But whatever their position, the greatest of these primary individuals were agents not just concerned with themselves. They kept something spiritually alive in them, as in a pocket of resistance, that could not survive in any other form or context.

> Handfuls of individuals rescued from forgetfulness were the harvest for the efforts of dozens of our missionaries ... These handfuls, these few, were enough to keep the link, the bond. But at what a cost![11]

In *Shikasta*, the first in her series of space fictions "Canopus in Argos," Doris Lessing offers in two dimensions what most Victorians had to struggle for in one. She imagines a fallen earth called Shikasta, overseen by a planet of wisdom, Canopus. That overview from a higher world was increasingly lost in the nineteenth century, in the growing dissolution of cosmological and theological structures and the establishment instead of a down-to-earth realism. But Doris Lessing restores that lost dimension in a subtle fashion, at once adding it at one level and taking it away at another. For as soon as Canopean agents come down to Shikasta to try to keep up "the link, the bond" between the two planets, they usually have to forget that they are from a higher world in order to work within the existing mental sets of human limitation. All that is left them on earth is a fitful, buried memory of some meaning and duty higher than they see around them. It is like Platonic reminiscence, faded, as the world gives way to a sort of daily realism, without the certainty of any validation from above itself.

Some agents lose their way, becoming assimilated and even ruined in the failure of their mission. One is a well-known public figure who in his youth had felt vaguely destined to achieve something. But unable to resist the temptations of fame and sex and drink in the fallen world's distortion of mission into ambition, he went blindly off course, unable even to acknowledge that there *was* a true course. There is hardly any one to tell him otherwise; the world will let him go on that way, losing himself *and* denying the loss, as if such was normal adulthood. And yet at times, aggressive or depressive, he is disappointed with what he has become – knowing he needs some awful disaster in order to come to himself and yet of course fearing and avoiding it. It is more frightening than straight despair; for in a way that Kierkegaard in *The Sickness Unto Death* thinks characteristic of the modern secular world, this is a man who, in denial, despairs of despairing. Yet his dreams make him wake in tears. His buried life has become a dream, a lost poem, some almost shameful, private form of subjective wishfulness without access to the objective status of reality any more. Doris Lessing's agents, I am saying, are like the great Victorian prophets in their lonely risks and individual ventures. And *Shikasta* is, among other things, like the view of the Victorians that they almost knew, or half-suspected, they could not take of themselves. They had to *be* themselves, instead, not certain of what they would look like from outside or above and what truth there would be from those perspectives. That was the "impossible" thought I pointed to in chapter 2.

George Eliot's Mordecai, a Jewish Carlyle in his desperately un-English vehemence, is accused of an insane egotistical exaggeration of his own value. Amidst the dying culture of cool England he will not think, humbly, "If not I, then another," nor will he be a modestly self-denying "Saint Anybody":

> The fuller nature desires to be an agent, to create, and not merely to look upon; strong love hungers to bless, and not merely to behold blessing. And while there is warmth enough in the sun to feed an energetic life, there will still be men to feel, "I am lord of the moment's change, and will charge it with my soul." (*Daniel Deronda* (1876), ch. 38)

An agent, a doer in the world: such a being risks everything, in the assertion of himself and of what, inseparably contained within him, he brings to the world.

One of these agent-individuals at the very limit of himself was John Ruskin, ending his strained life in madness. The universe is infinite and unfathomable, says Ruskin, but to "every human creature" there is some part of it that peculiarly seems his or hers, even a small part, like a hidden violet gathered from amidst the grass:

> One does not improve either violet or grass in gathering it, but one makes the flower visible; and then the human being has to make its power upon his own heart visible also, and to give it the honour of the good thoughts it has raised up in him, and to write upon it the history of his own soul. (*The Stones of Venice*, vol. 1 (1851), ch. 35, para. 5)

The "human creature" cannot respond to everything; there is too much for it in the great whole of creation. But the human creature becomes a "human being" when he or she charges with love and personality some partial thing that finds its value realized through that human agency. "This looks somewhat like pride; but it is true humility, a trust that you have been so created as to enjoy what is fitting for you."[12]

In such a spirit, doomed to misinterpretation, Ruskin entered a public room – and did so, not like the sort of political strategist that Hutton judged John Stuart Mill to be, but in a whirlwind, as though he were an event and not just a person. He could sound as arrogant and dogmatic as any Mordecai and would even secretly provoke and tease his audience with his individuality, in an effort to break through the social into the real and the personal.

He arrives at Bradford Town Hall April 21, 1864, invited by local dignitaries to give a talk on the best style of architecture for their new Exchange, and immediately he tells them, "I do not care about the Exchange – because you don't." They are rich businessmen who are going to spend £30,000, he tells them, and they think they may as well have the right thing for their money: "Now, pardon me for telling you frankly," he retorts, "You cannot have good architecture merely by asking people's advice on occasion."[13] Or he turns up to address the Royal College of Science in Dublin, May 13, 1868, politely told in advance that he may speak on anything at all except matters of religion. Immediately religion is what he begins with, refusing to have the most important of all concerns declared out of bounds. Why didn't he talk about art, as requested? "The main thing I have to tell you is, – that art must not be talked about ... The moment a man can really do his work he becomes speechless about it."[14] Or yet again, finally, a few months later he delivers the Inaugural Address to the Cambridge School of Art for Workmen, October 29, 1858:

> Perhaps some of my hearers this evening may occasionally have heard it stated of me that I am rather apt to contradict myself. I hope I am exceedingly apt to do so. I never met with a question yet, of any importance, which did not need, for the right solution of it, at least one positive and one negative answer ... For myself, I am never satisfied that I have handled a subject properly till I have contradicted myself at least three times.[15]

At *least* three times – every time propounding a different assertion with equal vehemence, absolutely sure of the truth of each in turn, as though each were like a different thought – no, almost a different person, at a different time – within him. If we are not inward with Ruskin on such occasions, we suspect him of being reactive and perverse – for we feel safer when personal identity is a form of predictable, repeated consistency. But really knowing a person means going beyond the literal, means being challenged into recognizing the extra dimension of himself signaled by tone. Ruskin tests the mechanically conformist social world by offering an almost violently direct version of himself unmediated by prior explanation or apology. It was emblematic of the need to have a society in which individuals could get what was within *out*, with a place for itself in the world. You may have heard I have a reputation for contradicting myself, Ruskin says, as though I were a logically feeble thinker. But to Ruskin, a sense of a mass of related contradictions is a holding-ground, a place in the very thick of content where some great issue is held together in search of the right formal resolution of its component parts. As he puts it in the last volume of *Modern Painters*, in response to the charge of having expressed in different parts of the work radically different views on the value of artistic "finish":

> All these passages are perfectly true ... The essential thing for the reader is to receive their truth, however little he may be able to see their consistency. If truths of apparently contrary character are candidly and rightly received, they will fit themselves together in the mind without any trouble. (*Modern Painters*, vol. 5 (1860), part 9, ch. 5, para. 22 fn)

You must trust particular dynamic thoughts, he says, at the moment they come to you, and with the force of absolute conviction. As agent for some message, you must trust yourself as a medium: you don't have to go into every situation trying consciously to remember what your principles are. For your principles are lodged in your passions. You can even trust the differences between the contradictory thoughts that arise on different occasions: they are independent proof that you haven't artificially willed the thoughts together, through the temptation to produce a fictive unity. Receive the truths *before* you look for their consistency, otherwise you will never see anything that is not immediately consistent with what you already think. Take each excited thought absolutely and on its own terms, in time. Only later will such thoughts shake down into finding their places relatively, as parts of a complex truth, within a whole too big for immediate understanding.

So it is that Ruskin writes thus in his address to the Cambridge School of Art, deploying a complex syntax that begins to combine two apparently contradictory absolutes from his own past thinking:

> You must not follow Art without pleasure, nor must you follow it for the sake of pleasure.

Ruskin's sentence is to do with what he elsewhere calls the great law of "reciprocal interference," a term he coins to indicate the way that colors are not single or separate but, when put together, modify each other.[16] It is like his law of help or brotherhood that applies when the sudden movement of a bird or horse has a phenomenal effect on all the landscape around it, or when the creation of an opening in the stone to let in a lovely light simultaneously creates a beautiful window-form in itself. In the space between the two modifying propositions – "not without, nor for the sake of" – the challenged reader or listener is left to infer the silent truth behind or beneath them. So it is in Turner when the imperfection of all the parts, viewed separately, drives the spectator to take in the whole. So it is too in the scriptures, notes Ruskin in a diary entry: "there are on every subject two opposite groups of texts; and a middle group, which contain the truth that rests between the others. The opposite texts are guards against the abuse of the central texts – guards set in opposite directions."[17]

This then is the role of the disturbing agent: to lodge within professional institutions all that defies professionalism and institutionalization; to stray beyond the politely formal remits of art criticism into morality, religion, and social politics; to represent a better world within this one. "There is a crust about the impressible parts of men's minds," Ruskin writes in *The Seven Lamps of Architecture* ("The Lamp of Power"), "which must be pierced through before they can be touched to the quick." This is the prophet who exists not to foretell the future, but to renew in the present the meaning of the founding spirit too often lost within the second-order literalness of habituation. You do not care about this Exchange, he says to his Bradford audience, so tell me what you do really care about: for "if a man is cold in his likings and dislikings, or if he will not tell you what he likes, you can make nothing of him." But if you tell me honestly what you like and love, I will know you – "What we *like* determines what we *are.*"[18]

Ruskin's most valuable contradiction was that he was a man of art who was also against "art." It was not merely that he was rude in lectures. He believed in *rudeness* in a deeper sense, in puritanical opposition to aesthetic polish. He loved not merely the rough but the rudimentary – the original vision and meaning, even if imperfect and unfinished. He loved the rough sketch that did not insist upon itself as art for art's sake, but honestly let you see *through* its means to the effect it gestured toward. This is like the prophet remembering the fundamental purpose when others do not even realize they have begun to take it for granted: he does not want to let art become a self-sufficient and smoothly orna-mental specialism; he will not allow art to forget that it exists for the sake of something of more primary significance than itself, to which it should devote all its means as secondary. That for Ruskin is the deepest meaning of realism, in its commitment of art to the truly real, to the given and to the created beyond us. Better the imperfections of some-thing aiming high than the perfectness of something merely lower.[19] "Better the rudest work that tells a story or records a fact," he writes in *The Seven Lamps of Architecture* ("The Lamp of Memory"), defending *unarty* art, "than the richest without meaning."

The first principle in his great chapter on "The Nature of Gothic" in the second volume of *The Stones of Venice* is "Savageness or Rudeness." In their wildness of thought and roughness of work, the great Gothic cathedrals have what Ruskin calls "a mountain brotherhood" with the great Alps. That the cathedrals are humanly raised to the maker of Nature is also to say that they are the expression of a great society envi-sioned within the mind of architects, leaving scope for their workmen to contribute creatively to the making of each part of the whole:

We have, with Christianity, recognized the individual value of every soul; and there is no intelligence so feeble but that its single ray may in some sort contribute to the general light. This is the glory of Gothic architecture, that every jot and tittle, every point and niche of it, affords room, fuel and focus for individual fire. (*The Stones of Venice*, vol. 1 ch. 21, para. 13)

Fire, individual fire. But if you want that heart and spirit, that life of the personal, you cannot also have mechanical perfection, smooth and easy integration, or even overall fairness. "For observe," says Ruskin, giving voice to the unashamed teacher within him: "I have only dwelt upon the rudeness of Gothic, or any other kind of imperfectness, as admirable, where it was impossible to get design or thought without it" (*The Stones of Venice*, vol. 2, ch. 6, para. 19). If you want the thought of a rough and untaught man, you have to have it in a rough and untaught way. At any cost, "*get* the thought, and do not silence the peasant because he cannot speak good grammar." Grammar and refinement are good things, both, only be sure of the better thing.

This is the great Ruskin who knows that imperfection is not merely a regrettable law of life but a great celebratory sign of vitality; who knows that strength and weakness are necessarily inextricable; who risks everything for the sake of one piece of what is genuinely and creatively good, rather than what is moderate, safe, and well balanced overall. I have sat at the outer edges of the councils of the judicious – at examiners' meetings, on boards of reviewers, at assessment interviews. For the most part, the members sit back unmoved, on their safe pairs of hands, detached and critical. The judicious are not looking for those who risk taking on more than they easily can. They are looking, unimaginatively, for the finished products whose limitations are banished to lie outside themselves, in all that they silently refuse to take account of, self-assured because self-enclosed. Cold judges themselves, the judicious would naturally prefer the cooler, safer perfectness of the lower, more mediocre nature.

But imagine instead an individual suddenly seized with a vehement passion for a great idea – that is what makes him or her suddenly individual:

> All his valuations are altered and disvalued; there are so many things he is no longer capable of evaluating at all because he can hardly feel them any more: he asks himself why he was for so long the fool of the phrases and opinions of others; he is amazed that his memory revolves unwearyingly in a circle and yet is too weak and weary to take even a single leap out of this circle. It is the condition in which one is least

capable of being just; narrow-minded, ungrateful to the past, blind to dangers, deaf to warnings, one is a little vortex of life in a dead sea of darkness and oblivion: and yet this condition – unhistorical, anti-historical through and through – is the womb not only of the unjust but of every just deed too; and no painter will paint his picture, no general achieve his victory, no people attain its freedom without having first desired and striven for it in an unhistorical condition such as that described. As he who acts is, in Goethe's words, always without a con-science, so is he also always without knowledge; he forgets most things so as to do one thing.[20]

This is Nietzsche, so *un*English in his romantic celebration of the un-ideal individualism of creative risk; yet *un*English in the sense that George Eliot's Mordecai or John Ruskin himself also were, in their defiance of their world. Matthew Arnold, in contrast, wanted disinter-ested many-sidedness and formal aesthetic adequacy, against the over-insistent ugliness of what was narrow. But this is precisely the diversity of the individual Victorian voices in fierce conversations characteristic of a time of transition when almost everything is up for grabs. For it is as though the whole is scattered amongst competing and conversing parts – the fault in one individual position balanced by recognition of it in another; the weakness in one part picked up by a corresponding strength in another. It is a great, struggling dialogue – the multi-logue that John Stuart Mill envisioned – as though all the great nineteenth-century figures were characters in some immense unwritten novel in search of a synthesis of itself, of one great human composite. There are not just conflicts, there are overlaps, and confusions, and subtly differ-ent personal emphases. But each viewpoint stands for something nec-essary to the (perhaps impossible) final whole – in a nineteenth century always troubled by the relation of parts and wholes, woods and trees. But here at least Nietzsche is much like Ruskin: he stands in fierce defense of the necessity of the part and the partial, when partial is what individuals almost inevitably have to be in order to achieve any-thing. Only: at that point of excitement, inside, they don't feel partial, they feel absolute, and undistinguishable from the belief they embody. The individual, with all that is more-than-individual inseparably within him or her, has to replace a lost society here – to compensate for a society that has forgotten something vital – with all the risk of personal distortion and impassioned egoism involved in the very attempt. The fair-minded, relativistic overview of what has been done is only for others, outside or afterward.

Outsiders could see in advance the way that John Henry Newman was going: to them it was entirely predictable that he would have to convert from Anglicanism to Roman Catholicism, in search of a greater defense for faith in a faithless age. But as Newman indicates in his autobiography, *Apologia Pro Vita Sua* (1864), from inside the experience it never felt so sure. It wasn't even clear it was a journey until afterward, and *then* it could not be wholly recalled. The man moved from position A beforehand to position C afterward, but the stumbling transition through B finds a letter or a name for itself only by means of a retrospect that is untrue to the undefinedly in-between experience of the time. It didn't feel as if it was anything. And now it is swallowed up in the end toward which it only eventually served as means. But what it really consisted in was all those implicit, microscopic circumstances "which the mind is quite unable to count up and methodize in argument" because they are "of a subtlety and versatility which baffle investigation."[21] Those inner subtleties and hidden underworkings are not events, though they eventually surface at the level of events: mentally, they constitute something that cannot be recalled within a specific narrative, being unassisted by outward settings. It is very odd when you ask gifted people how they have managed to become what they now are; or how they can do something you yourself want to follow. They cannot answer you properly, it seems:

> Things which are the most familiar to us, and easy in practice, require the most study, and give the most trouble in explaining; as, for instance, the number, combination, and succession of muscular movements by which we balance ourselves in walking, or utter our separate words … The longer any one has persevered in the practice of virtue, the less likely is he to recollect how he began it; what were his difficulties on starting, and how surmounted; by what process one truth led to another; the less likely to elicit justly the real reasons latent in his mind for particular observances or opinions.[22]

130

The *less* likely are such people to be able to give all their reasons, all their arguments, as from outside themselves, like a mere set of separate opinions, with the seemingly effortless logic of a John Stuart Mill. Their gradual autobiographical story, unknown at the time of its unfolding to be a story, has shaken down into implicit and personal character. "And over such of these it is," says Newman, in defense of these authentic inner knowers of life, "that the minute intellect of inferior men has its moment of triumph, men who excel in a mere short-sighted perspicacity." This is criticism's easy secondary triumph. It is the merely clever ones making the gifted look stupid. "What *exactly* do you mean?" they say, as Charles Kingsley asked Newman himself. And what I mean, replied Newman at the beginning of *Apologia Pro Vita Sua*, is not my words, my arguments, my actions, but ultimately "that living intelligence, by which I write, and argue, and act ... my mind and its beliefs and its sentiments."

The gifted ones can embody something, but often they cannot secondarily describe it or defend it as though from outside it. For they are not outside it. It is like the clamberer on a steep cliff "who, by quick eye, prompt hand, and firm foot, ascends how he knows not himself, by personal endowments and by practice, rather than by rule, leaving no track behind him, and unable to teach another."[23] If they were only allowed to make their attempts by telling their critics in advance exactly what they were going to do and how they were going to do it, they would never be allowed off the ground. But, riskily and magnificently, "it is a way which they alone can take; and its justification lies in their success." Nor can they teach the precise way afterward. There is no gap here between "ascends" and "how he knows not himself": not-knowing does not impede the act; it goes on in instinctive belief, the knowledge built into it. Newman writes a sort of suppressed poetry in his *University Sermons* using the bare force of words, unsupported by anything but themselves, to summon a store of mental experiences too swift, too interim and microscopic to be any other than latent in the mind.

There is a form of writing pitched between essay and sermon, in Ruskin, in Newman, which is not art but has learned from art, and seeks a strong language in defense of what is not simply explicable.

In Ruskin it is often summoned by the silent language of paint; in Newman by the invisible operations of mind. But in both it is what Carlyle in his great essay "Characteristics" (1831) calls "dynamical" rather than "mechanical" thinking. For wherever formal logic fails the gifted, art may exist to protect such gifts, to defend their existence – but it should not have to do so, alone. That is to say: it is important for the world that there is also within it a form of discourse, unconcerned with its own classification, which is no more and no less than the use of language to do thinking – which is not inventive art as such, or formal philosophy, and is not mocked for being neither. The climate that produced Victorian realist fiction also produced a non-fictional prose that pursued reality, equivalently, outside the novel.

This is why it is important that Newman does not accept as an inevitable irony that no real "doer" could write, or that no writer could truly "act." However much Newman says that language can do no more than give a relatively crude approximation of the subterranean workings of mind, he remains resolutely Victorian in still *trying* to do what he says cannot be wholly done – and, what is more, using the very difficulties themselves to express what they cannot quite overcome. Newman wants to be one of the few who is both intuitively right on the inside and able to defend himself from without. It is as great an aim in non-fiction as George Eliot's in the novel.

"Life-writing" is a currently trendy term for biography and autobiography; but actually to serve both realms, both life *and* writing, *and* make them serve each other, is a noble ambition. Art, history, theology, psychology, philosophy, science, culture, socio–economics, morality: a non–specialist, non–fictional prose existed to prove that these subjects should not be separate – were first of all individual thoughts and not just subjects – in the great human conversation.

★

In the *Westminster Review* for October 1863, there is an important but now little-known article in which S. H. Reynolds offered a contrast between Ruskin and Matthew Arnold, in terms of how each saw his vocation as "critic."

According to Reynolds, Arnold's sense of his proper duty as a literary critic was to pass disinterested impartial judgment upon the literature of each age viewed in relation to its own time and circumstance, and to pronounce accordingly upon its adequacy. But Ruskin's aim, said Reynolds, "is at once something more and something less than this." For Ruskin was different in two respects. First, he seemed far more personal than Arnold, less externally judicious, more partisan and more passionate in pushing the personal view to its limits. Second, for all Arnold's sense of himself as a failed poet, necessitating the shift to criticism in preparing the ground for a future great age of poetry, Ruskin was "rather perhaps an artist himself than properly a critic."

I say: here's to the creative reader, rather than to the critic. If the cultural mission is not to be pious and preachy, it has to be personal in voice and risk and nuance. I am glad of Ruskin's ruder ways – that often involuntary inability of his to keep the personal out; the impure mix of something artistic in writings that could not themselves claim the status of complete art. In the name of Ruskin, I celebrate those whose hybrid status is somehow in between categories, neither quite one thing nor another; who, rather than knowing beforehand, write to try to find out what they mean and what they are for; whose existence shows that there is a form of literary thinking, of creative thinking, that can go on outside literature, outside art. For these Victorian agents and prophets want not just a creative art-world but the human creativity of art also transferred back into the world itself.

That's why in our times, when too often the postmodern novel has been concerned with style, the Victorian realist inheritance has also gone into the writing of non-fiction and memoir. When I read John Berger's *A Fortunate Man* (1967) or Oliver Sacks's *A Leg to Stand On* (1984), what I find in writing sited between genres and between disciplines is an insistence on its sheer human content, not on formal artiness. Berger is writing about a real-life doctor who, making his work harder in all the imperfection of the higher endeavor, has implicitly taken into his vocation the skills of a novelist in order to seek to understand his patients from inside and not just treat them from without. Then Berger the novelist himself says of the doctor and his struggle to improve his small part of the world:

> I cannot evaluate that work as I could easily do if he were a fictional character. In a certain sense, fiction seems strangely simple now. In fiction one has only got to decide that a character is, on balance, admirable. Of course there remains the problem of making him so ... Now, by contrast, I am entirely at the mercy of realities I cannot encompass.[24]

At the mercy of realities is the right place for writing to be situated. It is the place Oliver Sacks likewise occupies when, as a doctor, he has to become so vulnerably a patient. His injured leg, apparently physically mended, is still somehow, at some other level, mysteriously unconnected to him, a dead weight. "Physician, heal *thyself*" is the challenge – and do so both from beyond medicine's existing competence and yet from within yourself. It is for Sacks a great and terrible experiment in putting the mind and body, the inside and the outside, back in synch again. We take these things for granted and live in second-order normality. But here in Sacks's trauma was the terrifying privilege of the lonely individual reliving in himself, as if for the first time again, all that went into the making and unmaking of fundamental human reality.

And I notice that, without my planning it, both these books are about medicine, about human health in the broadest sense. This leads to the final point I want to make in this chapter about "agents." We had a problem about what to do with the students who graduated from our part-time MA. In the case of many of them, we felt we had given them something revitalizing on the course, or enabled them to find their own buried lives. Then what? We had, it seemed, nothing to give them, nothing further for them to do in maintained pursuance, once they had graduated. It wasn't as if going on to a PhD and the whole business of specialized research was going to keep life up.

What gradually evolved of course was the idea that what we had tried to do for them, they should now go on to do for others. Graduates of the Victorian MA program were foremost amongst those who formed the organization "The Reader" and its Get Into Reading program on Merseyside, led by Jane Davis. It is a reading-group program offered to the ill, the redundant, the depressed, the elderly – where "reading group" does not mean exchanging secondary opinions *about* a book over a glass of white wine but the book itself being read aloud, in key places, making its real presence felt in the room. Then, at regular intervals, people speak in response, as though from somewhere deeper inside themselves than usual, which nonetheless for once can find a small society, an external community in which such innerness has a human home. I end here not with my own account but with the report of a visitor, a novelist and a poet and a writer of memoirs and factions, Blake Morrison:

The rise of book groups is one of the most heartening phenomena of our time, but this group is an unusual one, including as it does Viv and Chris from a homeless hostel, Michael who suffers from agoraphobia and panic attacks and hasn't worked for 15 years, Brenda who's bipolar, Jean who's recovering from the death of her husband, and Jan who has Aspergers. Some of the group are avid readers but for Chris, for example, it's his first experience of Shakespeare since school, and though the scene leaves him wanting to know what will happen next he's also baffled. "It's like music you've not heard before," others reassure him, "it'll get easier."

Under the umbrella of Jane Davis's Get into Reading scheme, there are now around 50 groups like this across Merseyside: groups in care homes, day centres, neurological rehab units, acute psychiatric wards, cottage hospitals, sheltered accommodation and libraries; groups for people with learning disabilities, Alzheimers, motor-neurone disease, mental health problems; groups for prisoners, excluded teenagers, looked-after children, recovering drug-addicts, nurses and carers; groups up to a maximum of ten people, since any more and there's no real intimacy. The educational background of the participants varies widely but there's no dumbing down in the choice of texts – *The Mayor of Casterbridge, Uncle Tom's Cabin, Rebecca, Great Expectations, Adam Bede, Sherlock Holmes, Jane Eyre, Of Mice and Men, Kes,* even Robert Pirsig's *The Art of Motorcycle Maintenance* among them. The usual pattern is for a complete book to be read aloud, cover to cover, at weekly sessions, which for a group spending an hour a week on a Dickens novel can mean six months devoted to a single book. Nobody is pressured to read aloud, but if and when they do the boost to their confidence can be striking.

These reading groups aren't just about helping people feel less isolated or building their self-esteem. Nor are they merely a pretext, in an area of high unemployment, for giving people the experience of working as a unit. More ambitiously, they're an experiment in healing, or, to put it less grandiosely, an attempt to see whether reading can alleviate pain or mental distress. ...

Perhaps the most convincing argument for the effectiveness of bibliotherapy comes from writers themselves. There's the case of George Eliot, for example, who recovered from the grief of losing her husband George Henry Lewes by reading Dante with a young friend, John Cross, who subsequently married her. "Her sympathetic delight in stimulating my newly awakened enthusiasm for Dante did something to distract her mind from sorrowful memories," Cross later wrote. "The divine poet took us to a new world. It was a renovation of life." John Stuart Mill enjoyed a similar renovation after the "crisis in my mental history" which he describes in his *Autobiography*, a crisis that began in the autumn of 1826 when "the whole foundation on which my life was constructed fell down [and] I seemed to have nothing left to live for." ...

As Thomas Hardy recognised, "If way to the better there be it exacts a full look at the worst." Hence Jane Davis's preference for classic texts which address existential concerns, not anodyne pep-ups. Medical staff attached to her scheme have occasionally worried that such and such a poem or passage might "make things worse." But what does "worse" mean when you're talking about people on a psychiatric ward? One geriatric patient burst into tears during a reading of Burns's "My love is like a red, red rose" – but insisted on staying there, through the tears, and professed herself "much better for it" afterwards.

Hardy's famous quote comes from a sequence of three poems, "In Tenebris," which he wrote in 1896–97, when his spirits were brought low by the excessive optimism of his peers. To Hardy, hell was other people being cheery – "the blot seems straightway in me alone ... / one born out of due time, who has no calling here." And yet he derives consolation from the very pessimism or "unhope" that weighs him down:

> Wintertime nighs;
> But my bereavement-pain

It cannot bring again:
Twice no one dies.

Each of Hardy's "In Tenebris" poems has an epigraph from the Psalms.
And far from being a simple glorification of God, the Psalms are often
engulfed by despair: "my heart is smitten, and withered like grass";
"attend unto my cry; for I am brought very low." Yet reading the
Psalms or Hardy or Gerard Manley Hopkins's "terrible sonnets" can be
cathartic. By attending to the cry of another, we articulate our own
cries, frame them, contain them, and feel better for it. Hector, in Alan
Bennett's *The History Boys*, puts it beautifully when he describes how,
in the presence of great literature, it's as if a hand has reached out and
taken our own. "I wake and feel the fell of dark, not day," Hopkins
writes, in his anguish:

> What hours, O what black hours we have spent
> This night! What sights you, heart, saw, ways you went!
> And more must in yet longer light's delay ...

Though Hopkins plumbs the depths he writes so searingly of his torment that the poetry becomes a cauterising iron to burn away our
own pain and to "leave comfort root-room" in which to grow.[25]

It is not only some of the texts but the whole spirit of this enterprise
that is the Victorian inheritance.

6

A Few of My Favorite Things:
A Glove, a Sandal,
and Plaited Hair

The Victorians were good at finding almost *anywhere* in time or space those tense areas that rang bells for themselves, echoing their concerns in excitement or in warning. Consciously immersed in history, without a clear sense of where its changes were leading them, the Victorians relished the chance to do with earlier times what they could hardly do in their own. In the clarity of retrospection, they loved to see in periods of great change both a dramatic analogy for their own predicament and a possible causal origin for it. Hence their imaginative visions of the great conflicts between pagan and Christian in the early centuries after Christ, or the decisive splits of the Reformation, or of the English Civil War. They were tough enough to know full well that it was a way of writing about themselves.

In this they owed much to the historical novels of Walter Scott. For Scott not only created the sense of two great oppositional forces, like past and future working out which should finally be which; he also placed in between them the smaller individual sentience of a wavering protagonist. The Victorian literary critic R. H. Hutton powerfully described what was at stake in the predicament of men such as Henry Morton in *Old Mortality* (1816), compromised in the midst of the fundamentalist conflict of Royalists and Covenanters, the Cavalier soldier Claverhouse and the Calvinist Balfour of Burley. Scott in himself preferred the extremes, Hutton notes, and was rather dismissive of these weak in-between characters created by the novelist in him:

in most of the situations Scott describes so well, his own course would have been that of his wilder impulses, and not that of his reason. Assuredly he would never have stopped, hesitating on the line between opposite courses as his Waverleys, his Mortons, his Osbaldistones do. Whenever he was really involved in a party strife, he threw prudence and impartiality to the winds, and went in like the hearty partisan which his strong impulses made of him. But granting this, I do not agree with his condemnation of all his own colourless heroes. However much they differed in nature from Scott himself, the even balance of their reason against their sympathies is certainly well conceived, is itself natural, and is an admirable expedient for effecting that which was probably its real use to Scott, — the affording an opportunity for the delineation of all the pros and cons of the case, so that the characters on both sides of the struggle should be properly understood.[1]

Scott's divided protagonists gave him "the instrument" he needed for displaying his insight into *both* sides of the public quarrel: those heroes are, Hutton concluded, "the imaginative neutral ground, as it were, on which opposing influences are brought to bear." They humanized that space and in so doing also enabled contemporary readers to take that bird's-eye view of the whole that they, like those in-between characters, could not take in their own time.

Among the fine neglected Victorian inheritors of Scott's model are Bulwer Lytton, especially in *The Last of the Barons* (1843), and Charles Kingsley in *Hypatia* (1853). In the latter, for example, a young monk hears within himself the smallest whisper of doubt, even as at the same time in another part of the novel an unbelieving philosopher is beginning to travel in the opposite direction, hearing a voice of faith. The skeptical whisper, "like the mutter of an earthquake miles below the soil," had "in that one moment jarred every belief, and hope, and memory of his being each a hair's breadth from its place." It was a tiny crack, which "was enough" gradually to make fissures in everything (*Hypatia*, ch. 9). For that hair's breadth is what makes for the novel-form itself, breaking up systems, opening life-shaking questions between character and belief.

For Lytton in *The Last of the Barons*, what one man (the Last Man of the Old Order) could do in the face of radical political change was part of a literary battle between genres – and what in the make-up of mankind those genres themselves represented – in the experimentalism of the novel-form. Everything goes in a novel. "History vies with romance in showing how far a single sword could redress the scale of war" (*The Last of the Barons*, book 12, ch. 6). In the defeat of Warwick, the great romantic individual fell and impersonal history triumphed: as in Scott, the feudal world began to give way to the modern one. But for Lytton this was like witnessing the working-out of the genetic future we have inherited from the past, in the mix of alliances and types, the conflict of old and rising classes, and the successful structures emergent from the struggle. It was not just looking back with hindsight: it was more like imagining, as a past itself could not, the future it turned out to have made for itself, unbeknownst, in our present. And likewise what our own present will become, and what effect *its* future will have in the reordering of the past, are equally beyond us in the continuing human process that we break up into "periods" only through need of explanatory convenience.

What was remarkable was the way in which some of these structures of historical fiction could be reworked within the domestic novel. The impressive novels of Mrs Humphry Ward, for example, often center upon a mixed marriage, such as her own parents had known – in *Helbeck of Bannisdale* (1898), between a staunch Catholic and the daughter of an unbelieving philosopher; in *Robert Elsmere* (1888), between Catherine, a woman of firm, ancient belief, and Robert himself, ever increasingly on his journey toward humanism and socialism. In such predicaments the spaces between the characters are as important as the characters themselves:

"I can believe no longer in an Incarnation and Resurrection," he said slowly, but with a resolute plainness. ...

His voice dropped to a whisper. She grew paler and paler.

"So to you," she said presently in the same strange altered voice, "my father – when I saw that light on his face before he died, when I heard him cry, 'Master, *I come!*' was dying deceived – deluded? Perhaps even," and she trembled, "you think it ends here – our life – our love?"

It was agony to him to see her driving herself through this piteous catechism. (*Robert Elsmere*, ch. 28)

The marriage almost ends here, though the bond of love struggles to endure, each partner endeavoring to be simultaneously true to the self and to the love between the selves. "As much tenderness between husband and wife as ever – perhaps more expression of it even than before, as though from an instinctive craving to hide the separateness below from each other and from the world" (ch. 37). It looks as if Catherine should simply be left behind, even though Robert cannot bring himself to do so – cannot wholly quit, as it were, the pre-Victorian for the sake of the modern and abandon the ancient faith for the sake of a new, secular, politicized freedom. The specific people and what almost allegorically they stand for are intermixed emotionally in such a novel. But that "tenderness" between them (in every sense of that word) may not be sufficient to hold them together any longer, may be merely a second-order mutuality in sympathetic and loyal pity that can do no more than paper over the cracks. In which case, there is a sense in which, ironically, Catherine can't simply be ditched but remains toughly right: that is to say, at some level, in its hard wiring, the novel has to agree with her that human feeling – even love and kindness and sympathy – may not be enough to stand as a raison d'être in place of belief or the want of belief. Victorian literature keeps asking us, anxiously, what is the future for humanism, when we are that future.

★

Here is one example of that future, itself anxiously looking back. In Philip Roth's *American Pastoral* (1997), the protagonist is known as "the Swede" because he is a Jew so assimilated as to have become more like a Scandinavian blond. One day, he gives a visitor to his factory a long talk about the family glove-making business, "Newark Maid." His detailed account of the sheer old-fashioned romance of his craft offers a distraction from his terrible present troubles with his anarchic daughter. It is a way of stepping back into the past and imitating his own father, the Jewish immigrant tanner amongst the Italian immigrant cutters, visualizing "how the skin is going to realize itself into the maximum number of gloves":

> "The skins all come in different according to each animal's diet and age, every one different as far as stretchability goes, and the skill involved in making every glove come out like every other is amazing. ... This cutting room is one of the last in this hemisphere. Our production is still always full. We still have people here who know what they're doing. Nobody cuts gloves this way anymore, not in this country, where hardly anybody's left to cut them, and not anywhere else either, except maybe in a little family-run shop in Naples or Grenoble. These were people, the people who worked here, who were in it for life. They were born into the glove industry and they died in the glove industry. Today we're constantly retraining people. Today our economy is such that people take a job here and if something comes along for another fifty cents an hour, they're gone." (ch. 4)

The production – handmade, high-quality, labor-intensive, time-consuming – belongs to an earlier age of traditional family businesses handed down from father to son. But in the mass, machine-manufactured markets of today "a product is a product ... The guy who makes them doesn't know anything about them." This is *American* pastoral: a hearkening back not to the idyllic woods and fields of Arden, but to an old-time animal-skin factory in New Jersey. "Are you the last of the Mohicans?" asks Rita, the Swede's audience. After all, what is celebrated is only the old-world luxury of ladies' leather gloves, and to the reader it may seem almost absurd that generations "were in it for life" – and not just life as duration, any more than work as mere money-making. Why spend your life on knowing gloves inside and out? They're not necessities but trivial luxuries from a bygone age. Yet it is also somehow disturbing that the product can now be mass-made in the modern world without anyone having to remember how or why it was originally done. It seems that in this secondary world of ready-made reproduction we have inherited inventions almost mechanically, like lives we have not in any sense earned but have taken for granted.

In the accelerated history of America, in the melting-pot of its diverse and intermingled races, changes that took up to three, four, or five generations in Europe, and still were fast enough to create unprecedented uncertainty, could happen suddenly within two – in the transition from pastoral to industrial, from craft to mass-production, from the work-ethic as vocation to job as mere income. In a novel such as Chaim Potok's *The Chosen* (1967) the shift from an ancient to a modern world, expressed in the movement from a father of strict religious orthodoxy to a son training to become a psychologist, can take place in a decade, racing through the impact of textual criticism of the Bible, of Darwinism, of Freud, as through books on the library shelves. This, I have been arguing, is the wider meaning of what in England we call "Victorian": the experience of feeling still situated *between* worlds – one of them previously firm but now near-dead and yet hauntingly missed; the other barely born, abruptly modern, and so strange and ungrounded as to seem closer to a loss than to a gain. In the midst of paradigm shift, it is realism in literature that struggles to create a holding-ground for the mingled elements of change and continuity.

Even a pair of gloves might serve, because in literary realism it is often the inner feelings that create value, rather than contemporary external status. In *American Pastoral* the gloves specially made for his visitor are delivered to the Swede for final inspection. For a minute or two, as in a brief lesson in apprenticeship, the thorough linguistic precision of detail irresistibly enlists attention – as though indeed this were important work:

> "See the seams? The width of the sewing at the edge of the leather – that's where the quality workmanship is. This margin is probably about a thirty-second of an inch between the stitching and the edge. And that requires a high skill level, far higher than normal. If a glove is not well sewn, this edge might come to an eighth of an inch. It also will not be straight. That's why a Newark maid glove is a good glove, Rita. Because of the straight seams. Because of the fine leather. It's well tanned. It's soft. It's pliable. Smells like the inside of a new car. I love good leather, I love fine gloves, and I was brought up on the idea of making the best glove possible. It's in my blood." (ch. 4)

If there was anything less than total experienced absorption in the cutting or the sewing, then there would simply be a small but ruinous mistake. That's all – *all* – it takes to make something into a love, a life, a world in which it becomes personally important to make as good a glove as possible. It simply demands, practically requires, all that mental attention and physical skill to do it.

This is how what Alasdair MacIntyre calls "practices," with defined functions, come into being and develop in the world. He defines a practice thus as any coherent and complex form of socially established cooperative human activity through which goods internal to that form of activity are realized in the course of trying to achieve those standards of excellence which are appropriate to and partially definitive of it.[2] In other words, merely to hit a ball with a bat, however skillfully, is not a practice; but the game of cricket or baseball is. It has rules, it has standards, and there are ways of getting things "right" that *internally* define what it means to be a "good cricket or baseball player." This is different from what might be called the *external* goods of status or money or power that, as extra, social rewards, may sustain the maintenance of practices but also corrupt them. We know of course that it is entirely possible to be a good athlete without being a good person – just as, on the other hand, it is equally possible that the qualities that go into being a good glove-maker may have transferable implications within the life as a whole, in terms of habits of discipline and commitment. In terms of that great Victorian question, "What am I *doing* with my life?" a practice offers justificatory defenses of itself, both in terms of its own internal requirements and through the sheer demands of time and effort it makes in keeping its adherents wholly occupied. Yet any practice can be a way of living in Plato's cave, in a place of temporary illusion cut off from the real light of the external world as a whole.

Perhaps that is all life is: the attempt to make existence so busy, so full, that it becomes an internal practice, keeping going by a kind of ongoing habit. In their continuance and their density, the novels of Trollope or Mrs Gaskell might almost convince a reader of the rightness of such patient immersedness in time. Except that always for the Victorian-minded, there is death, threatening the internal maintenance of a life with external considerations – considerations outside, beyond, and after the life of the individual, which even so turn back inside to haunt that life's self-sufficient security. You do your job, your specialism. With luck it matters to you within its terms, even though you might not be able to justify its existence if you were starting afresh under the eye of eternity. Otherwise you live for the freedom or the pleasure it buys after work and outside it. But for those who have the Victorian bump, there is a hangover of lost meaning, as well as a threatening nostalgia for definitive purpose.

The Swede sounds almost embarrassingly old-fashioned. If you met him in real life, you would inwardly groan at the banal attitudinizing, the opinionated generalities: certainly the novelist-figure in *American Pastoral* thinks this on first meeting him. But actually, beneath this normalizing cover, the inside story is that he wants his father's world because his own world is being painfully wrecked by his rebellious daughter. We get people wrong, says Roth: "You get them wrong before you meet them, while you're anticipating meeting them; you get them wrong while you're with them; and then you go home to tell someone else about the meeting and you get them all wrong again." The novelist in us might try to see that, but we can't all be novelists locking their study doors, "summoning people out of words and then proposing that these word people are closer to the real thing than the real people we mangle with our ignorance everyday." In fact, getting people right is not what life is about – writes Roth with poignant, rueful wit: "It's getting them wrong that is living, getting them wrong and wrong and wrong and then, on careful reconsideration, getting them wrong again" (ch. 1). A person can hardly live, continuously knowing that; but that's also why some write. It is the almost impossible awareness of those terrible ongoing mistakes that creates (in particular) the contrition of the realist novel and also makes it uncomfortably self-interrogating.

Yet there are sudden moments when the writing also hits something unexpectedly real, or real in unexpected ways, and feels "right." It is not in the notional themes, conventional categories, or opinionated generalizations but in what may be genuinely minute and tiny that the real justification of a life can begin to be felt. "Slowly, slowly," the Swede urges his customer, "always draw on a pair of gloves by the

fingers … afterward the thumb, then draw the wrist down in place …
always the first time draw them on slowly … Close your hand, make
a fist":

> "Feel how the glove expands where your hand expands and nicely
> adjusts to your size? That's what the cutter does when he does his job
> right – no stretch left in the length, he's pulled all that out at the table
> because you don't want the fingers to stretch, but an exactly measured
> amount of hidden stretch left in the width. That stretch in the width is
> a precise calculation." (ch. 4)

The good sign is in how involved the language is, crafted itself by what
it refers to: "nicely adjusts," "hidden stretch," "precise." For a split
second, it feels like that moment when a glove was first made. It is also
a little version of the room that might be still left for personal individual reality in the world, getting it just right, making it fit. At that point,
perhaps it does not matter that it is only a glove or that the Swede is
not himself its maker. One of the few things Tolstoy admired in *King
Lear* was the dying old man at the end unable even to undo "a button."
Glove-making is work – that great nineteenth-century belief – that
this man is holding onto, for a sense of life's value and purpose. Ruskin
says to the craftsman who is not an artist that humans are sent into the
world to do their work and to do it with all their might. And perhaps
all that humans do, Ruskin says, is finally and inevitably in the eye of
eternity "useless in itself," because meant instead "for nothing more
than the exercise of the heart and of the will" (*The Seven Lamps of
Architecture* (1849), ch. 5, para. 24). To Ruskin's God, what really matters
may be the ostensible means – the content and the effort and the emotion along the way – even when to ourselves we had supposed it was
all for the sake of a specific, locally targeted end. But it would take the
external perspective of a God to offer that reassurance – that it was not
what you did but what you put into it. And simultaneously the need
for that God and the felt possibility of his non-existence are part of the
Victorian experience that continues to be inherited, with different
nuances, in particular individual experiences. Thus Ralph Waldo Emerson
in his essay on "History," first given as a lecture in 1836: "There is a

relation between the hours of our life and the centuries of time": the latter, ostensibly so much bigger, may be contained, re-enacted, and reworked even within the experience of the former.

So this chapter asks finally: where do you find the Victorian bump *now*? And for all my admiration of the authors, my first answer must be: *not* be by looking at those explicitly neo-Victorian novels self-consciously based on Victorian characters such as John Fowles's *The French Lieutenant's Woman* (1969), A. S. Byatt's *Possession* (1990), or Graham Swift's *Ever After* (1992).

I find it in certain moments of personal experience – every time there is a shift in ordinary, basic life from secondary to primary reality. I mean: those shifts of realization that come with the death of a parent, a divorce, redundancy or job-frustration, problems with an adolescent child, a medical diagnosis. For example, if not *Possession*, then Stephanie giving birth in A. S. Byatt's *Still Life* with an almost Tolstoyan power (1985). It need not necessarily be trouble or getting people wrong – it could be joy, surprise, getting people right for once, an ostensibly small incident; but the intrinsic seriousness that says "this is it, this is primary" is often what comes out of trouble or at least arises out of the felt contrast with trouble or with neglect. And then it is not so much that the world has changed utterly as that it has become realized again as what it really, really always was at some level, while you were going along taking it for granted, as humans normally must.

And I find it also in certain times or places. For one, in the Jewish-American novel from the second half of the twentieth century onward – in its inheritance of what Arnold called Hebraic seriousness in a secularized context; in its immigrant blending of Russian influence, Tolstoy and Dostoevsky, with that of English Victorians such as George Eliot and Hardy; in its assimilation of these rich stores within the great melting-pot of American experience, accelerating history, compressing different races, re-forging new and old. The classic example is Bernard Malamud's *The Assistant* (1957), *Crime and Punishment* translated into the smallness and poverty of lower-class Brooklyn:- the story of Frank Alpine, the Italian-American robber of a Jew's grocery store who returns in contrition to try to make a second life for himself as an assistant within it. "With the idea of self-control came the feeling of the beauty of it – the beauty of a person being able to do things the way he wanted to, to do good if he wanted; and this feeling was followed by regret – of the slow dribbling away, starting long ago, of his character." A reviewer may speak of the book's "old-fashioned humanity," but when like Frank you have never had it, there's nothing old-fashioned, nothing secondary or to be taken for granted, about it. Some authors, through the felt needs of their characters as individuals, passionately refuse to admit either fashion or cliché. "What an extraordinary thing he thought: you could be not moral, then you could be." "His confession deeply moved him. What an extraordinary only human thing to be in love!" To such as Frank – the ones from below who have gone without or made a mess, all their lives – morality itself could be not only hard but *beautiful*, the ethical also movingly aesthetic as a forgotten achievement, giving form to what had repeatedly been ugly and broken in a life. "He planned to kill himself, at the same minute, had a terrifying insight: that all the while he was acting like he wasn't, he was really a man of stern morality."[3] "Like he wasn't he was," carved out of the very midst of the sentence, is the Malamudian shorthand for the beginnings of a redemption that recreates not only Frank but what in *Women in Love* Lawrence's Birkin had called "the old, old effort at serious living" itself.

There are other places I shall come to in a moment where, between one life and another, old forces stir again to see if there is room or form for themselves in a new world. But what these cases share is a sense of transition – always personal, even when social and historical – and a determination not to find the easiest way through that transition, but to hold on to as much as possible of what is at stake within it: literature as the human melting-pot, or a human holding-ground, are the metaphors I have used throughout this book.

★

It should be no surprise then that the last great, formally Victorian novel is Rudyard Kipling's *Kim*, published in 1901, the year of the queen's death, but set in India. For it is in India that Kipling finds what he must have thought was the center of the world, the center of life, in its full multifariousness, matched by the youthful Kim's own lively mixture of identities. "India was awake and Kim was in the middle of it, more awake and more excited than any one … he borrowed right- and left-handedly from all the customs of the country he knew and loved" (ch. 4). It is not like E. M. Forster's *A Passage to India*, published in1924, for there the caves are empty, and in *Kim* the world is full. What in another novel of the late-nineteenth/early-twentieth cen- tury would be disillusionment becomes this in Kim, re-entering the world after the illness that left the "unnerved brain" edging away from all outside:

> He did not want to cry, – had never felt less like crying in his life, – but of a sudden easy, stupid tears trickled down his nose, and with an almost audible click he felt the wheels of his being lock up anew on the world without. Things that rode meaningless on the eyeball an instant before slid into proper proportion. Roads were meant to be walked upon, houses to be lived in, cattle to be driven, fields to be tilled, and men and women to be talked to. They were all real and true – solidly planted upon the feet. (ch. 15)

It is a fundamental simplicity that is re-won in that penultimate sen- tence – "Roads … houses … cattle … fields … men and women …" – a sentence that seems to be naturally set up to go, to spell itself out in the basic grammar of life. And it is Irving Howe, the great writer on Jewish assimilation in America, who best describes the generosity of the novel. Howe focuses in particular on the relationship between worldly Kim and the innocent, other-worldly Buddhist lama, as incongruous companions along the way: "Part of the pleasure that *Kim* engages is that of accepting, even venerating sainthood, without at all proposing to surrender the world, or even worldliness, to saints. *Kim* embraces both worlds, that of the boy and the lama, the senses and beyond, recognizing that anyone who would keep a foot, or even a finger, in both of these worlds must have some discipline in adjust- ment and poise."[4] The greatest moment in the book is when, on the verge of what he believes to be the final goal of nirvana, the lama for- goes his longed-for transcendence. In a complex mixture of the invol- untary and the willed, so characteristic of the book, the holy man forces himself to return to the human earth below, for the sake of the boy. "Then a voice cried; 'What shall come to the boy if thou art dead?' and I was shaken back and forth in myself with pity for thee" (ch. 15). The two ways of contemplation and action, of the soul and the world, are not reconciled – only, in between them, the boy and the old man. That's the rich human area, with issues and alternatives still unresolved on every side, which is full of the matter "the Victorian bump" flourishes upon. So it is bitterly ironic that Kipling should be dismissed as imperialist by critics specializing in what has become known as postcolonial studies. For what Victorian literature gave the world was not so much an imperialist ideology as the very opposite: a form for holding together vital split-off elements that it would be only too easy to separate one way or another; a saving opportunity for elements that somehow need to stay together, even in their contradictions, for the sake of something in their midst that is better than is ever offered by mutually weakening alternatives. That is why we are not just talking about a historical predicament that may recur at different points of transition in different places but will always pass. What is at stake here is a stubborn and loyal structural commitment in the middle of things, a not letting go of what may not come together and yet should not go apart: the particular and the general, the religious and the secular, the old and the modern, the human world of freedom and the need still for something more.

Moreover, *Kim* is a sign here that it is not just amongst the Jews of Brooklyn and Newark but amidst a wide variety of the exiles and the second-generation children of immigrants that the sense of being between two worlds is still acutely realized. It underlines how misleading are the critical histories when the multicultural novel, so often labeled "postcolonial," can as aptly be described as a Victorian descendant. It is structurally not surprising, for example, that a novel such as Helen Oyeyemi's *The Icarus Girl* (2005), about the "half-and-half" child of an English father and a Nigerian mother, should first take place in England, then move back to Nigeria where Jess finds her other half, and finally return to England, with that other half battling her for her identity in a *Wuthering-Heights*-type struggle that combines Nigerian magic with English psychotherapy. It is that third

150

phase when the pieces are held together that is the most powerful one. Thus, Nadeem Aslam's *Maps for Lost Lovers* (2004) holds the bitter inner conflicts of a Pakistani family within the tense bounds of a northern English town. The politicized, westernized father; the traditionalist Muslim mother; the children in confused reaction against their complex inheritance – all this makes for a novel lodged painfully not only between ancient and modern, but between an England and a Pakistan that coexist in this single mixed place. It is like a modern *Robert Elsmere*, a renewed *Sons and Lovers*, struggling for an almost genetic orientation. Nor is it simply a coincidence that a novel such as Xiaolu Guo's *A Concise Chinese-English Dictionary for Lovers* (2007), the tale of a Chinese girl-student adrift in London, should be written in an invented in-between language, existing in a floating present tense. Struggling with the language and its people, the protagonist notes that in Chinese there are no changes of mood or tense. Perhaps English reality does not comprehend how the universe continues always in the present tense. Or perhaps she must learn that "love" becomes more conditional, more time-limited in English, and all too far away from remaining the infinite state of being she dimly recalls as her birthright.

★

But I have held something back. Philip Roth's novel is not just about a glove manufacturer. The visitor to the factory turns out to be a sinister figure who has been leading the Swede's daughter toward a sort of 1960s anarchic protest against bourgeois America, culminating in a bomb assault. My question is this: what if, quietly and safely, it *was* a novel about a parochial glove-maker, and his family, without the surrounding drama and disaster? Would that be interesting now, as it might have been when realism was essentially new to the nineteenth century? Or would it be precisely the worn-out, bourgeois thing that the Swede's daughter assumes it is?

Great events inspire interest. They can still justify the claims of realism as an act of witness and record. *Half of a Yellow Sun* by Chimamanda Ngozi Adichie, published in 2006, is a plainly unremitting novel about the Nigerian civil war and the brief existence of Biafra as an

151

independent republic of the Igbo people between 1967 and 1970. To the world that watched but did not intervene, this was a country that disappeared – now barely a memory; once no more and no less than a nightly horror on the television screens, with a million people lost in starvation and genocide. But the novel begins in comfortable safety before the secession, in a thoroughly Europeanized setting amidst afflu-ent, radical, university people. Ugwu, a 13-year-old from a poor village, becomes a houseboy in the home of a lecturer, the charismatic Odenigbo, and his sophisticated girlfriend Olanna. "You will eat meat every day," his aunt tells Ugwu as she wins him the position. He lives in a western-ized luxury he does not take for granted, is taught English, and reads the books in the house. In particular he loves Frederick Douglass's memoir of what it was like to be a slave in nineteenth-century America.

And then comes the catastrophe that plunges them all into another world – the sort of unimaginable disaster, like the revenge of ancient forces, that an émigré writer such as Joseph Conrad fearfully stood for. Conrad, that harbinger of the twentieth century and its horrors, con-ceiving of civilized life as a thin, barely cooled layer of molten lava that at any moment might break and plunge the unwary walker into the fiery depths below.[5] The Nigerian soldiers come and lay waste the house. The civilized comfort of a previous age is gone. But it is too hard, too much, to take in. Only, in the aftermath, a single stylish sandal lies on the ground, leather straps and thick wedge heel. And Ugwu "imagined the chic young woman who had been wearing it, who had discarded it to run to safety" and "wondered where the other sandal was."[6] It is just a small detail, but a resonant as well as manageable one.

Half of a Yellow Sun has within its cast of characters one figure in particular who is ideally qualified, it seems, to record the violent devastation that ensues. Richard Churchill is a liberal English jour-nalist who, trying to lose his outsider status, writes a series of alerting articles, which he intends to turn into a book on the crisis, its injus-tice, and the terrifying loss of humanitarianism. But the chronicler that the novel actually throws up for itself has to be a more half-and-half figure: it is not Churchill, it is Ugwu, who begins to find scraps of paper secretly to record, in the English he has learnt, all that he has seen and heard. And there is a vital turning-point for Ugwu in this, when he writes, really writes, as if for the first time and knows the purpose of the ability. It happens at a moment of refuge in the midst of the Civil War, when Olanna is simply plaiting the hair of the sick and fragile baby she has had with Odenigbo. The normal little action makes her remember something almost unbelievably horrific that she saw on a train amidst people desperately fleeing invasion: it was a mother with her child's severed head in a box, all she could keep of the remains. Olanna continues to comb Baby's hair, and again, as on previous occasions recently, some of it falls out – no one and nothing is healthy now:

> Olanna placed the comb down. "I keep thinking about the hair on that child's head I saw on the train; it was very thick. It must have been work for her mother to plait it."
> "How was it plaited?" Ugwu asked.
> Olanna was surprised, at first, by the question, and then she realized that she clearly remembered how it was plaited and she began to describe the hairstyle, how some of the braids fell across the forehead. Then she described the head itself, the open eyes, the greying skin. Ugwu was writing as she spoke, and his writing, the earnestness of his interest, suddenly made her story important, made it serve a larger purpose that even she was not sure of ... (ch. 34, pp. 409–10)

A little later she remembers a fragment from a destroyed poem by their old friend, the poet Okeoma, killed in the war. It was something about placing pot upon pot to form a ladder to the sky and try to make the sun rise when it refuses to do so: "'Clay pots, fired in zeal, they will cool our feet as we climb.' ... It was my favourite line. I can't remember the rest" (p. 411). But those pots go untransformed, and the details of the hair-plait are similarly unimportant, if there is not some-one attending who sees in them that "larger purpose that even she was not sure of." It is "the earnestness" of Ugwu's attention – that old-fashioned word – that suddenly made the story important.

But where does importance come from? It is good that Olanna is not sure of quite *why* Ugwu's listening so intently to her makes the story matter more. If she was sure that its purpose was to "remember

Biafra," then it would be too public and too principled too soon. But if it wasn't Biafra, and if it wasn't a dead child, and if there was nobody there who believed the ordinary little details of glove or plait to be worth recording ... then what?

Then (let me face the thought) Victorian realism is probably a dead end? And a dead end because without a catastrophe that no one could possibly want, ordinary life in the West (we might fear) lacks significance, has been getting worn out. We might re-enliven our own English interest with a Nigerian, a Pakistani, a Jewish, or a Chinese perspective on things, brought in from the diasporas without. But that sounds dubiously secondary and decadent. If Biafra – and a century of equivalent disasters that shake nineteenth-century humanism and make it seem all too nineteenth-century – is the true measure of what is really real, then our half-guilty liberal interest in it is not up to that measure, and not admirable for needing the witness of those extremes.

In *More Die of Heartbreak* (1987) one of Saul Bellow's earnest protagonists, talking to his mother amidst the famines of Somalia, thinks also of the Russian concentration camps of Solzhenitsyn in contrast with the condition of smaller and safer lives in the prosperous West, with its little, safe, lyrical poems of daily life.

> Educated opinion in the USA envies the East its opportunities for more cultivation and development because *there* they suffer more deeply. Here suffering is trivial. Nobody gets hacked to pieces for his ideas. ... Russian suffering was, in a large historic view, suffering in its classic form, the suffering mankind has always known best in war, plague, famine and slavery. Those, the monumental and universally familiar forms of it, must certainly deepen the survivors humanly.

But, thoroughly bored with the idea of the Decline of the West, sick of its disloyalty to itself, he also wants to say something else:

> My temptation was to try to make Mom understand that the sufferings of freedom also had to be considered. ... Inside the sealed country, Stalin poured on the *old* death. In the West, the ordeal is of a *new* death. There aren't any words for what happens to the soul in the free world.[7]

154

It is with that new death and that equivocal suffering, denied even the dignity of those old nouns, that the great Jewish-American realist novels of the twentieth century – Bellow's own *Herzog* (1964), Bernard Malamud's *Dubin's Lives* (1979), Philip Roth's *The Counterlife* (1986), and Joseph Heller's *Something Happened* (1971) – do battle, in all their experimental twists and turns and returns, their intense repetitions, and their insistent linguistic richness. "It is my wife," says Heller's man – throwing at her all the terrible sprawling things he has secretly thought of her – "maudlin, discouraged, repetitious, often inane"; testing, without quite letting himself know it, whether there is anything left in him after all these bad things are let out. "It is my wife," he says, still going on, "my wife, of all people," who (with all her faults, and his disclaimers) at one moment of crisis in the family *can* suddenly make him see aright and feel straight again.[8] Heller has worked hard to resist the charge that this is merely recourse to old-fashioned sentimentality (the usual complaint), and to insist, almost despite himself, that the good feeling does have a real place in the world.

But realism may well fail if our reality is doing so. An art that hides that possibility in inventive ingenuity is no art but camouflage and cosmetics. It only encourages (and barely defers) the loss of belief in the reality that we do have. Unless, however, the case is this: that realism no longer serves us rightly because it has become a style and an attitude, a false framework without sufficient imaginative vision left in it to capture the really real that might be there, occluded by our now-dulled norms. Realism has always made itself deliberately vulnerable to those self-interrogations, those self-doubts, which also are its own investigative tools. It was George Eliot's classic formulation: if we had a keen vision and feeling of all merely ordinary human life, it would be like hearing the grass grow or the squirrel's heart beat – it would be too much, we could not stand it, we would die of that roar that lies on the other side of silence. So perhaps we can only safely function by registering 5 percent of reality, *and* by having to think that is all there is. But the best realist novels know that though they may only raise that habitual level by a few vital points, the difference these novels make is greater than the few extra percent they manage, for opening up the imagination to still more than themselves. George Eliot herself surrendered some of the perfections of *Middlemarch* to write *Daniel Deronda* in desperate experimental search for something better to believe in a decaying England.

Deronda himself will risk almost anything, will sacrifice all that he tiredly knows too well, for the sake of what he calls emotional knowledge – something that stirs him to life in a dying world. He will even risk believing in the visionary Jew Mordecai, though there is always a very good chance that a prophet is no more than a crazy man. George Eliot's was not a completed task in this final novel, and there was no automatic handover to successors (and not even any guaranteed successors) in the risk of lost insights. Perhaps completion or solution are too much to ask of art, and others will turn to politics or to religion instead. But the Victorians do ask too much of art: Dickens, finding a powerful area, puts into its holding-ground more and more and more human material until it yields him some suddenly emergent realization. A poet may find some sort of opening, in a language that can work away from large canvases and excessive demands. But without epic, without a modern myth, without the equivalent of Wordsworth's long poem *The Prelude* to show what the poetry means in a life, it is the novel that seeks to put such openings into working human forms, to see what they mean in practice.

I do not think for one moment that I know "where we are now," which poets or novelists might help us – if indeed there is a "we" or an "us"; if indeed literature can be supposed to be of help in relation to so-called reality. I would be a fool to say Victorian Literature Still Matters Because – say – it can offer us Salvation. I don't believe so, any more than I believe that everything that has happened in modernism or postmodernism is either to be erased or made into a Victorian inheritance. I begin much further down than that, in the partial and personal, the admittedly autobiographical, in the smaller individual areas where I think I do know something of where I am or at least of what worries or moves me. There, I think I cannot do without what the Victorians stand for, however roughly approximate my sense of that is and however vulnerable to the tiresome charge of undue essentiality. Why can't one do without the Victorian reality-bump? Because

I believe it is a proper default setting, a basic sense of the ordinarily real from which to start. That doesn't mean that it is wholly true, somehow 100 percent reproductive of reality. We today are often sophisticated in skepticism. So what? The best Victorian realists knew full well what they were doing was only approximative; it didn't stop them – what else could they do? – for they were tough.

Where we do differ from the Victorians, it seems to me, is that we do not want and do not believe in authoritative guidance. We do not trust a prophetic Ruskin using medieval architecture to point to lost structures forgotten by a later material world. In the late 1970s and into the 1980s, Doris Lessing created in her space fictions new ways of seeing the world; but for all the recent award of the Nobel Prize, it has been largely possible to ignore her.

Yet Doris Lessing only ever went into space in order to come back to earth. The wise authority in these novels comes from the planet Canopus, in its struggle to maintain the health of the universe. But in the second of the series she concentrates on Canopus's lesser semblance, the planet Sirius, with its technological empire and its bureaucratic administrators. Here is one agent from Sirius who is beginning to see more than her role allows. She is describing how through technology the Sirians had created seemingly perfect worlds, without any work to do, without any problems to solve, without want or need for effort: it is like a vision from the young John Stuart Mill. And this achievement in fact turned out to be a death sentence:

> We did not foresee that these billions, not only on our Home Planet but also on our Colonised Planets, would fall victim to depression and despair. We had not understood that there is inherent in every creature of this Galaxy a need, an imperative, towards a continual striving, or self-transcendence, or purpose.

There was random violence and widespread neurosis as a result. The bureaucracy sought remedies:

> One was a phenomenon that became known as "invented usefulness." Once the cause of the general malaise had been understood, there were various solutions suggested, of which this was the first attempted: areas

157

that had been relinquished to machines and technical devices were deliberately reclaimed. I will mention one example. Everything to do with the supply and demand of food, and household goods, had been mechanised so that the means in most general use everywhere in the Empire were vast depots, each one of which might supply a million inhabitants, needing no attendants at all. These were dismantled in favour of small suppliers, sometimes specialist suppliers, and the billions employed in this artificial industry were conspicuously happier than the idle masses. For a time.

Then it was that, for all the expedients designed to paper over the cracks, the administrators found that they were dealing with an underlying *law* – namely:

> That where the technology exists to accomplish a service or task or to supply a need, then if this is not used, because of humanitarian or other social reasons, there is no real or lasting satisfaction for the people involved in that sector. They all *know*, in the end, even if this realisation is delayed – sometimes deliberately, and by themselves, in efforts of self-deception – that their labours, their lives, are without real purpose.[9]

With her double perspective, Doris Lessing requires us both to see these people and also to be them, a powerful demand at the levels of both cool objectivity and warm imagination that the reading of fiction exists to serve. No *real* satisfaction, without *real* purpose. The fundamental existential problem for Sirius is summed up in one question, "What for, what are we for?" It is what William James in the chapter on "The Sick Soul" in *The Varieties of Religious Experience* called the great question of those who need to be twice-born, who need to find another level of meaning in life before death comes: "Why? Wherefore? What for?" The deeper souls panic early, but in the end potentially every individual existence, says James, "goes out in a lonely spasm of helpless agony." Tolstoy was one of those "primitive oaks of men" unsatisfied by the superficialities of time.[10]

I am saying that the question "What for?" is what arises out of and is addressed back toward the Victorian bump. I mean: the realist tradition is rightly still *the* default position, the bedrock sense of common existence. It may be wrong; it certainly cannot be wholly truthful. It may be too dualistic, rendering too sharply the boundary between self and others, inside and outside, and leaving an idea of the self at once too small and too separate. But I still think it is right to start from it, again and again, as what we have and what at the very least we need to reform if we can. Because it is *that* basic model that provokes the questions: what *more* do we need than this? What *other* if this gets the nature of reality wrong? Why Victorian literature still matters is because it is like Thomas Hardy: nothing is worth believing unless it can overcome the obstacles, the objections, the sufferings that Hardy reluctantly represents in his very existence. Or because it is like how it is for Adam Bede in that passage I brought out near the end of chapter 1: that whatever else happens around or beside it in the world, there still remains the physical reality and separation of Hetty Sorel.

I have not been saying that everything that matters is "Victorian." And however much this book is implicitly averse to the Joycean view of art that goes from *Portrait of an Artist* to *Ulysses* to *Finnegans Wake*, I do not wish that modernist and postmodernist experimentalism should be wiped from the pages of literary history. What I want to say is that for people such as me, at any rate, the experiments and the questionings have to be directed back toward the default position, the holding-ground inherited from Victorian realism in all its variations, if there is to be genuine change.

And here is a last example of what I mean. Unsuccessfully for some years now, I have been trying to convince others that Bernard Malamud's *Dubin's Lives* is the great novel of the second half of the twentieth century – written twenty years after *The Assistant*, but in the speed of American modernization from almost a whole generation later. It is the novel in which Malamud said he put everything he knew about writing and about marriage, in middle age, and followed the tradition of George Eliot and Thomas Hardy.

Dubin himself is a writer, working on a biography of D. H. Lawrence even though it would be closer to his own temperament were he writing the life of Hardy. But Lawrence challenges Dubin, disturbs him, pushing him, just as he pushed the Victorians, into all that goes on, neglected, within the deep, physical realm of primal being. And as a consequence within his life, or as an experiment for his work, Dubin the married man has a quasi-Lawrentian affair with a young woman, close to the age of his own daughter. It is a common little story in itself. But in the novel not only does the affair damage the marriage; its failure also seems to create in Dubin a writer's block. In a kind of chaos, the writing disturbs the life, the life the writing, till ironically through their mutual failure neither is separate from the other in the terrifyingly dense confusion of realism's vicious circles. It is the stuff, William James would say, that all conversions come out of.

But no conversion or solution comes. For years the man has taken his customary long run or walk, especially when in trouble with his work: now, when suddenly the winter snow comes down, he misses his customary way, loses himself, risking his life without meaning to: "The wild begins where you least expect it, one step off your daily course. ... Am I where I think I am?" Later, in spring, he goes back to see where or how he went wrong, but finds that "where he had been was in truth no longer there."

Whatever the conventional forms and notional themes of Dubin's life, the content is *more* than them, is unsatisfied by them, fires a rich language and a sense of meaning that cannot be wholly contained in them – and yet cannot find anything else beyond them. That is realism on the brink, holding all the rich content amidst all the questions and the needs. Says Dubin, "I want my life to tell me what it knows."[11] This Blackwell Manifesto says: amen to that.

Notes

Introduction: The Victorian Bump and Where to Find It

1 Christina Rossetti, "Later Life," 1880, sonnet 6; Thomas Carlyle, *Chartism*, 1839, "Condition-of-England Question."
2 Philip Davis, *The Victorians*, vol. 8 of the *Oxford English Literary History* (Oxford: Oxford University Press, 2002).
3 See John Ruskin, *The Stones of Venice*, 3 vols., 1851–3; vol. 1, ch. 2, paras. xi–xii; vol. 2, ch. 6, para. xii.
4 Lloyd Jones, *Mister Pip* (London: John Murray, 2007), pp. 110–12, 133.
5 J. H. Newman, "Who's to Blame?" in *Discussions and Arguments*, 1872.
6 A version of chapter 2 appeared in *The Reader*, 21 (Spring 2006) and in Clare Williams and Victoria Morgan (eds.), *Shaping Belief* (Liverpool: Liverpool University Press, 2008); a version of part of chapter 5 appeared in *The Reader*, 16 (Autumn 2004) and was reprinted in the *Ruskin Review*, 1 (no.1, Michaelmas 2004).
7 See www.thereader.co.uk and www.getintoreading.org.

Chapter 1 Victorian *Hard* Wiring

1 See George Steiner, "Critic"/"Reader," in Philip Davis (ed.), *Real Voices on Reading* (Basingstoke and London: Macmillan, 1997), pp. 3–37.
2 John Stuart Mill, *Autobiography*, 1873, ed. J. Stillinger (Oxford: Oxford University Press, 1971), p. 81 (ch. 5).
3 Iris Murdoch, *Metaphysics as a Guide to Morals* (London: Chatto and Windus, 1992), p. 146.
4 See the introduction above, p. 5.
5 Ludwig Feuerbach, *The Essence of Christianity*, 1841, trans. Marian Evans [George Eliot], 1854 (New York, Evanston, and London: Harper Torchbooks, 1957), p. 82 (ch. 8).

6   Feuerbach, *The Essence of Christianity*, p. 47 (ch. 3).

7   *The George Eliot Letters*, ed. Gordon S. Haight, 9 vols. (New Haven: Yale University Press, 1954–78), vol. 4, pp. 300–1.

8   John Morley, *Nineteenth-Century Essays*, ed. Peter Stansky (Chicago: University of Chicago Press, 1970), p. 309 ("The Life of George Eliot" also reprinted in Morley's *Critical Miscellanies*, 1888, vol. 3)

Chapter 2   Isaiah and Ezekiel – But What About Charley?

1   *William Blake*, ed. M. Mason, Oxford Authors (Oxford: Oxford University Press, 1988), p. 13.

2   John Stuart Mill, *Autobiography*, 1873, ed. J. Stillinger (Oxford: Oxford University Press, 1971), pp. 83–4 (ch. 5).

3   Ludwig Feuerbach, *The Essence of Christianity*, 1841, trans. Marian Evans, 1854 (New York, Evanston, and London: Harper Torchbooks, 1957), p. 64 (ch. 5).

4   *Lux Mundi*, ed. Charles Gore (London: Murray, 1889), p. 18.

5   Carlyle, "Characteristics," 1831, in his *Critical and Miscellaneous Essays*, 7 vols. (London: Chapman and Hall, 1869), vol. iv, p. 1.

6   See *Clough: Selected Poems*, ed. J. P. Phelan (London: Longman, 1995), p. 141.

7   Roma Notebook, quoted in *Clough: Selected Poems*, ed. Phelan, p. 15.

8   George MacDonald, *Wilfrid Cumbermede*, 1872, second edn. (London: Strahan, 1873), ch. 42, p. 354. Further references to this edition are hereafter cited after quotation in the text.

9   *Newman's University Sermons 1826–43* (London: SPCK, 1970), p. 215 (sermon 11).

10 See Søren Kierkegaard, *The Sickness Unto Death*, 1849, trans. H. V. and E. H. Hong (Princeton, NJ: Princeton University Press, 1980), pp. 84–5, where Kierkegaard offers the analogy of a day laborer being summoned for reward, unbelievably and undeservedly, by the mightiest emperor in the world.

11 William James, *The Will to Believe and Other Essays*, 1897 (London: Longman, 1915), pp. 54–5. Further references to this edition are hereafter cited after quotation in the text.

12 William James, *The Varieties of Religious Experience*, 1902, ed. M. E. Marty (Harmondsworth: Penguin, 1985), p. 55. Further references to this edition are hereafter cited after quotation in the text.

13 William James, *Selected Writings*, ed. G. H. Bird (London: Everyman, 1995), p. 17. Further references to this edition are hereafter cited after quotation in the text.

14 Roberto Mangerbeira Unger, *The Self Awakened: Pragmatism Unbound* (Cambridge, MA: Harvard University Press, 2007), p. 1.

15 George MacDonald, *A Dish of Orts* (London: Sampson Low, Marston, 1893), pp. 4, 254. Thoughts are not ours, says MacDonald, they come from somewhere and mean more than we know. For MacDonald that somewhere is God. Whatever things we write about are really thoughts embodied in the world: "It is God's things, his embodied thoughts, which alone a man has to use, modified and adapted to his own purposes, for the expression of his thoughts" (*A Dish of Orts*, p. 320). That source is why a person's work, even one thought, will always mean more than he or she intended, more than he or she can control: "A man may well himself discover truth in what he wrote; for he was dealing all the time with things that came from thoughts beyond his own" (*A Dish of Orts*, p. 321).

16 *The Personal Notebooks of Thomas Hardy*, ed. R. H. Taylor (London: Macmillan, 1978), p. 89.

17 John Dewey, *Philosophy and Civilization* (New York: Minton, Blach, 1931), p. 120.

18 "And we cannot be honest unless we recognize that we have to live in the world *etsi deus non daretur*. And this is just what we do recognize —before God! God himself compels us to recognize it. So our coming of age leads us to a true recognition of our situation before God. God would have us know that we must live as men who manage our lives without him. The God who is with us is the God who forsakes us (Mark 15.34). The God who lets us live in the world without the working hypothesis of God is the God before whom we stand continually. Before God and with God we live without God. God lets himself be pushed out of the world on to the cross. He is weak and powerless in the world, and that is precisely the way, the only way, in which he is with us and helps us. Matt. 8.17 makes it quite clear that Christ helps us, not by virtue of his omnipotence, but by virtue of his weakness and suffering."

Chapter 3 Not So Straightforward: Realist Prose and What It Hides Within Itself

1 Charles Dickens, *A Tale of Two Cities*, 1859, book 2, ch. 5.
2 Charles Dickens, *Oliver Twist*, 1838, ch. 44.
3 *Oliver Twist*, ch. 46.
4 *Oliver Twist*, ch. 46.
5 *Oliver Twist*, preface.
6 Charles Dickens, *Bleak House*, 1853, ch. 8.
7 *Bleak House*, ch. 15.
8 Herbert Spencer, *Essays on Education*, 1860 (London: Dent, Everyman, 1910), pp. 165 ("Progress: Its Law and Cause"), 329 ("On the Origin and Function of Music").

9 For the beginning of this experimentation see Philip Davis, *Shakespeare Thinking* (London: Continuum, 2007), pp. 92–5.

10 Doris Lessing, *Under My Skin* (London: HarperCollins, 1994), p. 218.

11 *The Autobiography of Margaret Oliphant*, 1899, ed. Elisabeth Jay (Oxford: Oxford University Press, 1990), p. 37.

12 *The Autobiography of Mrs Oliphant*, p. 21.

13 Ian McEwan, *Saturday* (London: Vintage, 2006), pp. 67–8.

14 Thus Bernard Malamud, writing in the 1960s: "People have forgotten how to write vertically, there is so much horizontal writing" (Library of Congress, Malamud papers, II.13 folder 11).

15 John Stuart Mill, *Utilitarianism and Other Essays*, ed. Alan Ryan (London: Penguin, 1987), pp. 146, 150–1 ("Bentham").

16 Quoted in Robert D. Richardson, *William James: In the Maelstrom of American Modernism* (Boston and New York: Houghton Mifflin, 2006), p. 152.

17 Herbert Spencer, *The Principles of Psychology*, first published 1855, 2 vols. (London: Williams and Norgate, 1881), vol. I (1881), p. 151.

18 For Middleton's brand of realism, see in particular his *Valley of Decision* (London: Hutchinson, 1985) and *An After-Dinner's Sleep* (London: Hutchinson, 1986).

Chapter 4 A Literature In Time

1 *The Letters of Mrs Gaskell*, eds. J. A.V. Chapple and Arthur Pollard (Manchester: Manchester University Press, 1966), pp. 602, 541.

2 *Anthony Trollope: The Critical Heritage*, ed. Donald Smalley (London: Routledge and Kegan Paul, 1969), p. 147 (review of *Orley Farm*, *Spectator* (11 October 1862), my italics).

3 *Anthony Trollope: The Critical Heritage*, p. 304.

4 Anthony Kenny, *Will, Freedom and Power* (Oxford: Blackwell, 1975), pp. 70, 91–2.

5 *Anthony Trollope: The Critical Heritage*, p. 537.

6 *Anthony Trollope: The Critical Heritage*, p. 304.

7 Edmund Burke, *Reflections on the Revolution in France*, 1790, ed. C. C. O'Brien (Harmondsworth: Penguin, 1978), p. 120.

8 *Anthony Trollope: The Critical Heritage*, p. 304.

9 Douglas Oliver, *Poetry and Narrative in Performance* (Houndmills, Basingstoke: Macmillan, 1989), p. 107 (my italics).

10 Cf. Arthur Hugh Clough with different times on different lines, the lines nonetheless syntactically interacting in ways that stretch the brain beyond separate times – when "the feeling is not with me now / Which will I know be with me presently" ("Dipsychus," part 2, sc. 5).

11   Walter Bagehot, "Wordsworth, Tennyson, and Browning; Or Pure, Ornate and Grotesque Art in English Poetry," 1864, in *Literary Studies*, ed. R. H. Hutton, 2 vols. (London), vol. 2, p. 338.

12   *The Letters of Robert Browning and Elizabeth Barrett 1845–6*, 2 vols. (New York and London: Harper & Brothers, 1899), vol. i, pp. 407, 211; vol. ii, p. 54; vol. i, pp. 181–2.

13   *The Reader*, 27 (Autumn 2007), p. 30.

Chapter 5   Individual Agents

1   See Benedict de Spinoza, *Ethics*, trans. George Eliot, ed. Thomas Deegan (Salzburg: Salzburg University, 1981), pp. 151–2.

2   Saul Bellow, *Herzog*, 1964, (Harmondsworth: Penguin, 1976), p. 189.

3   Saul Bellow, *Humboldt's Gift*, 1975 (Harmondsworth: Penguin, 1976), p. 431.

4   See Schwartz's "Poetry and Belief in Thomas Hardy" in *Hardy: A Collection of Critical Essays*, ed. A. J. Guerard (Englewood Cliffs, NJ: Prentice-Hall, 1963), esp. pp. 128–31.

5   Ian Hamilton, *A Gift Imprisoned* (London: Bloomsbury, 1998), p. xii.

6   *Middlemarch*, ch. 58.

7   George Henry Lewes, *The Life and Works of Goethe*, 1855 (London: Everyman, J. M. Dent, n.d.), p. 176 (book iii, ch. 6).

8   See Andrew Pyle (ed.), *Liberty: Contemporary Responses to Mill* (Bristol: Thoemmes Press, 1994), p. 207.

9   R. H. Hutton, *A Victorian Spectator*, eds. R. H. Tener and M. Woodfield (Bristol: Bristol Press, 1989), p. 231. Newman's comments on literature as the personal use of language are to be found in *The Idea of a University* (1852, revised 1859, 1873), II ("University Subjects"), ii ("Literature"), sec. 3.

10   *Spectator*, December 7, 1895.

11   Doris Lessing, *Shikasta* (London: Jonathan Cape, 1979), p. 111.

12   *The Stones of Venice*, vol. 1, ch. 2, para. 17.

13   "Traffic" in *The Crown of Wild Olive*, paras. 52–3.

14   "The Mystery of Life and its Arts," *Sesame and Lilies*, lecture 3, paras. 1–2.

15   In *On the Old Road*, in *The Library Edition of the Works of John Ruskin*, eds. E. T. Cook and Alexander Wedderburn, 39 vols. (London: George Allen 1901–12), vol. 16, p. 177 ff.

16   *The Stones of Venice*, vol. 3, ch. 1, para. 26.

17   *The Library Edition of the Works of John Ruskin*, vol. 5, p. liii.

18   "If a man is cold in his likings": *Stones of Venice*, vol. 1, ch. 2, para. 12; "What we like": "Traffic" in *The Crown of Wild Olive*, para. 61.

19   *The Stones of Venice*, vol. 2, ch. 6, para. 11.

20 Friedrich Nietzsche, *Untimely Meditations*, trans. R. J. Hollingdale (Cambridge: Cambridge University Press, 1983), p. 64 ("On the Uses and Disadvantages of History for Life").

21 John Henry Newman, *University Sermons 1826–43*, eds. D. M. Mackinnon and J. D. Holmes (London: SPCK, 1979), p. 257 (sermon 13, 1840, "Implicit and Explicit Reason").

22 Newman, *University Sermons 1826–43*, pp. 83–4 (sermon 5, 1832, "Personal Influence, the Means of Propagating the Truth").

23 Newman, *University Sermons 1826–43*, p. 257 (sermon 13, 1840, "Implicit and Explicit Reason").

24 John Berger, *A Fortunate Man*, 1967 (New York: Vintage, 1997), pp. 158–9.

25 Blake Morrison, "Are Books the New Prozac?" *Guardian* (Review section), January 5, 2008.

Chapter 6 A Few of My Favorite Things: A Glove, a Sandal, and Plaited Hair

1 R. H. Hutton, *Sir Walter Scott*, English Men of Letters (London: Macmillan, 1878), ch. 10.

2 Alasdair MacIntyre, *After Virtue* (London; Duckworth, 1981), p. 175 (adapted).

3 Bernard Malamud, *The Assistant* (Harmondsworth: Penguin, 1967), pp. 141, 157; *A New Life*, 1961 (Harmondsworth: Penguin, 1968), pp. 189, 223.

4 "The Pleasures of *Kim*," reprinted in *Kim*, Norton Critical edition, ed. Z. T. Sullivan (New York: Norton, 2002), p. 329. On the Jewish immigrant world, see Irving Howe's *World of Our Fathers* (New York: Simon and Schuster, 1976): "Insofar as the Yiddish intellectuals continued in the path of their own tradition, they could not open themselves sufficiently to the surrounding cultures of Europe and America, nor engage themselves sufficiently with the values of modernity to which they now and again aspired. Yet insofar as they accepted the secular cultures of their time, they risked the loss of historical identity, a rupture with that sacred past which could stir the sceptics almost as much as the believers. The culture of *Yiddishkeit* – at once deep-rooted and precarious, brilliant and short-breathed – had always to accept dilemma as the ground of its existence. It had always to accept the burden of being at home neither entirely with its past nor entirely with the surrounding nations. Out of its marginality it made a premise for humanness" (p. 18).

5 The description is from Bertrand Russell's memoir of Conrad in his *Portraits from Memory* (1956).

6 Chimamanda Ngozi Adichie, *Half of a Yellow Sun* (London: Harper Perennial, 2007), p. 203 (ch. 18).

7   Saul Bellow, *More Die of Heartbreak* (London: Secker and Warburg, 1987), pp. 99–101.
8   Joseph Heller, *Something Happened* (New York: Knopf, 1971), pp. 185–6.
9   Doris Lessing, *The Sirian Experiments* (London: Jonathan Cape, 1981), pp. 14–15.
10 William James, *The Varieties of Religious Experience*, 1902, ed. M. E. Marty (Harmondswoth: Penguin, 1985), pp.153, 186.
11 Bernard Malamud, *Dubin's Lives* (London: Chatto and Windus, 1979), pp. 149, 151, 191, 294.

Index